The Ridgeway Path

Seán Jennett

Long-Distance Footpath Guide No 6

London Her Majesty's Stationery Office

Published for the Countryside Commission

Front cover: Avebury Circle
Frontispiece: Avebury from the air (*Aerofilms Ltd.*)
Back cover: Uffington White Horse
Endpaper: Ridgeway Path near Letcombe Bassett

The maps in this guide are extracts from Ordnance Survey maps
1:25,000 or about 2½ inches to 1 mile, and have been prepared from
O.S. Sheets SU16, 17, 27, 28, 38, 48, 58, 68, 69, 79,
ST70, 80, 90, 91

Drawings by John Western
Nature drawings by Harry Titcombe

© Crown copyright 1976
First published 1976

Government Bookshops

49 High Holborn, London WC1V 6HB
13a Castle Street, Edinburgh EH2 3AR
41 The Hayes, Cardiff CF1 1JW
Brazennose Street, Manchester M60 8AS
Southey House, Wine Street, Bristol BS1 2BQ
258 Broad Street, Birmingham B1 2HE
80 Chichester Street, Belfast BT1 4JY

Government publications are also available through booksellers

**Long-Distance Footpath Guides published for the
Countryside Commission by HMSO:**
The Pennine Way by Tom Stephenson: 120 pages, £2·50 net
The Cleveland Way by Alan Falconer: 144 pages, £1·80 net
**The Pembrokeshire Coast Path by John H. Barrett:
124 pages, £2·50 net**
Offa's Dyke Path by John B. Jones: 124 pages, £2·50 net   ⎫ **to be**
Cornwall Coast Path by Edward C. Pyatt: 120 pages, £2·50 net   ⎬ **published shortly**

Countryside Commission
John Dower House, Crescent Place
Cheltenham, Glos. GL50 3RA

Prepared for the Countryside Commission
by the Central Office of Information 1976

Printed in England for Her Majesty's Stationery Office by Ebenezer Baylis & Son Ltd.,
Worcester and London. ISBN 0 11 700743 9 Dd. 288820. Pro. 3868. K80 7/76

Maps

The waymark sign is used in
plaque and stencil form
by the Countryside
Commission on long-distance
footpaths

Maps reference

Class 1 Road		A40(T)
„ 2 „	Fenced	B4010 Unfenced
Roads Under Construction		
Other Roads	Good, metalled	Poor, or unmetalled
Footpaths	FP Fenced	FP Unfenced
Railways, Multiple Track	Station Road over FB	
	Sidings	Tunnel (Footbridge)
„ Single Track	Level Crossing Embankment	
	Viaduct	Road under
„ Narrow Gauge		

Aerial Ropeway .... *Aerial Ropeway*

Boundaries, County or County Borough

„ „ „ „ ʼ „ with Parish

„ Parish

Pipe Line (Oil, Water) .... Pipe Line

Electricity Transmission Lines (Pylons shown at bends and spaced conventionally)

Post Offices (in Villages & Rural Areas only) .... P	Town Hall ..... TH	Public House *PH*
Church or Chapel with Tower ▟	Church or Chapel with Spire ▟	Church or Chapel without either ●
Triangulation Station .... △	on Church with Tower ...... ▵	without Tower ▵
Intersected Point on Chy ..... ○	on Church with Spire ... ○̇	without Spire ●	on Building ■
Guide Post ... *GP.* Mile Post ..... *MP.*	Mile Stone ..... *MS.* Boundary Stone ... *BS* ○	Boundary Post *BP*○
Youth Hostel .... **Y** Telephone Call Box (Public) .. **T**	*(AA)* **A** (RAC).. **R**	Antiquity (site of) ... ✛

Public Buildings .... ▰	Glasshouses ▰
Quarry & Gravel Pit	Orchard
National Trust Area (Coombe Hill NT)	Furze
Osier Bed	Rough Pasture Heath & Moor
Reeds	Marsh
	Well .... W ○
Park, Fenced	Spring .... Spr ○
Wood, Coniferous, Fenced	Wind Pump .... *Wd Pp.*
Wood, Non-Coniferous Unfenced	
Brushwood, Fenced & Unfenced	

Contours are at 25 feet vertical interval, shown broken in built up areas.

Spot Height .... *123 ·*

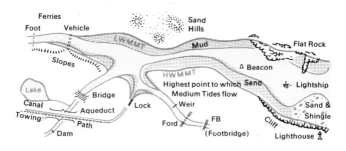

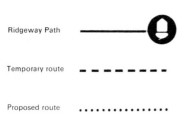

Ridgeway Path

Temporary route

Proposed route

Addresses for further information

The Nature Conservancy Council (South Region), Foxhold House, Thornford Road, Crookham Common, Newbury, Berks.: for Fyfield Down and Aston Rowant National Nature Reserves.

Berkshire, Buckinghamshire, and Oxfordshire Naturalists' Trust (BBONT), Hon. General Secretary, P. G. Hodgson, Shirburn Lodge, Watlington, Oxon: for the nature reserves of Happy Valley, Chequers Knap, Chinnor Hill.

Natural History Museum, London: for plant-ecology wall charts, especially No. 3 Chalk Grassland.

The National Trust, 42 Queen Anne's Gate, London SW1H 9AS: for details of its properties (and of membership).

Author's acknowledgements

The following organisations have supplied information and I am grateful for their kindness:
National Trust; Nature Conservancy; English Tourist Board; Berkshire, Buckinghamshire and Oxfordshire Naturalists' Trust (BBONT); Cyclists' Touring Club; British Horse Society; County Councils of Berkshire, Buckinghamshire, Oxfordshire, Hertfordshire, and Wiltshire; Jacob Sheep Society; Central Electricity Generating Board, S.W. Region (Didcot); Institute for Research on Animal Diseases; Atomic Energy Research Establishment (Harwell).

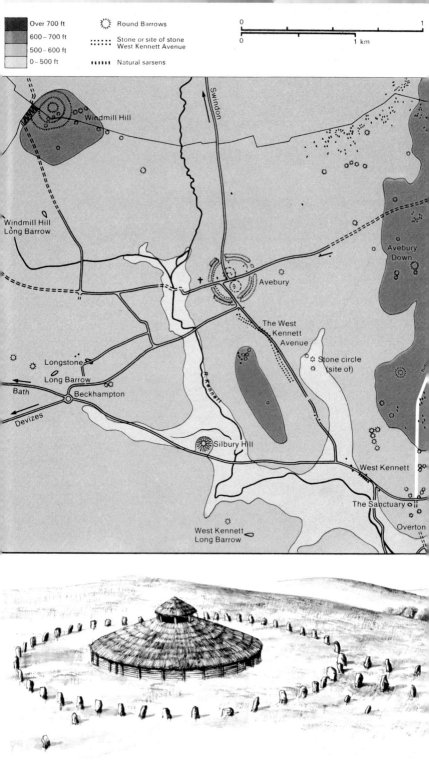

Over 700 ft

Round Barrows

600 – 700 ft

Stone or site of stone
West Kennett Avenue

500 – 600 ft

0 – 500 ft

Natural sarsens

0

1

0

1 km

Swindon

Windmill Hill

Windmill Hill
Long Barrow

Avebury
Down

Avebury

The West
Kennett
Avenue

Longstone
Long Barrow

Stone circle
(site of)

Bath

Beckhampton

Devizes

Silbury Hill

West Kennett

The Sanctuary

Overton

West Kennett
Long Barrow

The long-distance footpath

The Ridgeway long-distance footpath, planned under the terms of the National Parks and Access to the Countryside Act of 1949 and of the Countryside Act of 1968, and implemented by the Countryside Commission, was opened on 29 September 1973. This period, fourteen months after the route received approval by the Secretary of State for the Environment, may be compared with the fourteen *years* it took for rights of way on the Pennine Way to be negotiated and approved. The problems on the Ridgeway Path were neither as numerous nor as intractable, but the rapid completion of this path is perhaps an illustration of the impetus that has been achieved.

The conception of a route along the Chilterns and the Wessex Ridgeway as a long-distance footpath was expressed in 1947 in the Report of the Special Committee on Footpaths and Access to the Countryside (the Hobhouse Committee) (Cmd 7207). Among other long-distance paths the report recommended the creation of one that might run along the Chiltern ridge to Wallingford, along the Wessex Ridgeway to Avebury, and then across the Vale of Pewsey, passing Warminster, Cerne Abbas, and Lambert's Castle, to reach the sea at Seaton Bay. In 1956 a line from Cambridge to Seaton Bay submitted by Tom Stephenson of the Ramblers' Association was considered by the National Parks Commission. By 1962 the Commission had decided on the preliminary route, which would have crossed nine counties. It was decided to start with the Berkshire, Oxfordshire, and Buckinghamshire sections and consultations and joint surveys with the local authorities went ahead. These were continued from 1966 with Hertfordshire to link up two sections in Buckinghamshire across an intervening piece of Herts. In the same year it was decided to extend the investigations to include the Wiltshire section of the Wessex Ridgeway as far as Avebury. The proposal for the present route was submitted to the Secretary of State for the Environment in December 1971 and approved in July 1972. There are at present no plans to extend the path at either end.

The opening ceremony took place on Coombe Hill on 29 September 1973. The path was declared open by Lord Nugent of Guildford and the official party then led a walk down into Wendover.

The long-distance path as finally approved extends for 85 miles from Overton Hill near Marlborough and Avebury to Ivinghoe Beacon near Tring. It passes through five counties—Wiltshire,

Top (opposite): The principal prehistoric monuments of the Avebury region.
Below (opposite): Reconstruction of the Sanctuary as it might have appeared c. 1600 B.C.
(With acknowledgements to the Royal Archaeological Institute)

Berkshire, Oxfordshire, Buckinghamshire, and Hertfordshire. The recent changes in county boundaries have transferred some sections between Scutchamer Knob and the Thames from Berkshire to Oxfordshire, but they have not otherwise affected the path.

The path provides a few new rights of way, but for the greater part the various stretches of bridleway and footpath that make up the long-distance path have been open to the public for many years—indeed for many centuries, for it is probable that parts of the path, notably the Wessex Ridgeway and the Icknield Way, have been in use for more than four thousand years. What is new is the provision of suitable connecting links and the designation and protection of the path as a permanent facility for the enjoyment and the recreation of the public.

To this end it has been signposted and waymarked throughout. The signposts are of oak, with lettering in low relief on the arms, and the waymarks are either low concrete 'plinths' with the word 'Ridgeway' on them or, away from roads, the Countryside Commission's white acorn signs. These acorn waymarks are sometimes low-relief plaques nailed in place, but more often are simple stencilled symbols to be found on stiles, gates, posts, and tree-trunks. Commonly the acorn stands upright, but occasionally, and unofficially, as an indication of direction, it has been stencilled sideways.

The long-distance footpath seeks as much as possible to avoid the use of surfaced roads, and to this end it occasionally makes a detour from what appears to be the more direct line.

The path is divided into two nearly equal parts by the river Thames between Streatley and Goring. The two parts are dissimilar in character. The western part, from Overton Hill to Streatley, largely follows the line of the neolithic upland track known since at least Anglo-Saxon times as the Ridgeway and marked as such on modern Ordnance Survey and other maps. Most of this is a distinct and unmistakable track, seldom hindered by overgrowth or obstruction, swinging along mile after mile between widely spaced fences or hedges—so widely spaced that the available 'freeway' is as great as that of many motor roads. It is a coherent, distinct, and distinctive track. Its name has been applied to the long-distance footpath as a whole, though in fact the part of the path east of the Thames had not previously been known as the Ridgeway.

Prehistoric travellers on the Ridgeway crossed the Thames and continued their journey towards the east coast along the track that long afterwards became known as the Icknield Way or Icknield Street—the word 'street' should not mislead you into supposing that the Icknield Way is Roman. Whereas the Ridgeway has remained unsurfaced for nearly all its length, the Icknield Way has in many places become surfaced motor road, as inconvenient for walkers as motor roads usually are. In order to avoid these surfaced stretches in drawing the line of the long-distance footpath, various local footpaths have been used as connecting links.

The salient differences between the two parts of the long-distance path, east and west of the Thames, are therefore the unified character of the west and the somewhat piecemeal and more varied character of the east, the very few stiles or gates in the west, and the frequent stiles and gates in the east. Whether you enjoy one more than the other is a matter of personal preference. Each has its charm and its details of interest.

The two parts require to be named distinctly, since it would be confusing to refer to them both as 'the Ridgeway'. In this book, when distinction is required, the western part, since it passes through Wessex, will be called the Wessex Ridgeway, and the eastern part the Icknield track.

This, the seventh of the Countryside Commission's long-distance footpaths to be opened, is different from the two earliest ones, the Pennine Way and the Cleveland Way. Whereas the first two run over bleak and wild highland areas, the Ridgeway Path runs over country that nowhere attains a thousand feet, and for the greater part is at a considerably lower level. Though the climate in the winter may be very cold and the weather windy, the Ridgeway Path is less tough than the hills of the north. Walking the Ridgeway long-distance path requires no exceptional endurance, if marathon feats of distance walking are not attempted, and no more care than is sufficient to ensure your warmth and dryness. There are no precipices to fall over, no crags to be climbed. The principal perils are probably a strained ankle from the frequent ruts, and perhaps in summer too much exposure to the sun.

Story of the Ridgeway

The long-distance footpath of the Countryside Commission runs for 85 miles from Overton Hill west of Marlborough to Beacon Hill near Ivinghoe in Buckinghamshire. It is based on two very ancient highways, the Wessex upland way known as the Ridgeway, which goes down to the Thames at Streatley, and the Icknield Way, which continues the line north-eastwards from Goring on the east bank of the Thames, opposite Streatley. Between Goring and Streatley there must once have been a ford or some other easy crossing of the river.

These 85 miles by no means represent the whole of the ancient highway. The Ridgeway continued south from Overton Hill, through the village of East Kennett, to cross the Wansdyke and pass between the tumulus known as Adam's Grave on Walker's Hill and the neolithic camp on Knap Hill to Alton Priors. It crossed the Vale of Pewsey and went on to Salisbury Plain and Stonehenge. It is believed to have continued into Dorset and to the sea.

At the other end of the long-distance path the Icknield Way went from Ivinghoe Beacon north-eastwards through Cambridgeshire to Grime's Graves in Norfolk, and from there to the coast of the North Sea.

Palaeolithic man

Much of the route of the Ridgeway and of the Icknield Way is apparent on the ground. Even if it were not so we should have to assume that some such way must have existed, for it led to neolithic and Bronze Age centres of such magnitude and importance that it is difficult not to believe that people travelled to them not only from all parts of Britain but probably from the Continent as well. Avebury and Stonehenge are not matched anywhere in Europe and it is scarcely credible that they could have been built by a local tribe merely for local use.

Why should visitors and pilgrims to these notable shrines have come along the Icknield Way and the Ridgeway? Perhaps because these highways already existed and had done so from times beyond the memory of men. The reason for this assumption lies in the geography of the southern half of England. The ancient highways keep to the chalk ridges, and the chalk country extends in a forked figure, as it were a £ sign, north-eastwards from Dorset. It divides to pass south of the Thames valley towards Eastbourne and Dover, and north of that valley through Wiltshire, Berkshire, Oxfordshire,

Experimental barrow on Overton Down. Photographed when the barrow was dug in 1960, vegetation has now almost completely re-established itself.

Buckinghamshire, Hertfordshire, and over Cambridgeshire into Norfolk.

In order to understand the importance of the chalk we must imagine an England very different from that of today. In prehistoric times the plains and lowlands were covered with thick forest and undergrowth, in which men found progress difficult or impossible. The chalk uplands provided going that was drier underfoot and less impeded by vegetation.

The English Channel is of comparatively recent geological age—it is no more than about eight thousand years since the waters of the sea broke down the chalk connection with the Continent to make Britain an island. Long before that time palaeolithic or mesolithic men, following their food-gathering and hunting mode of life, could readily have wandered from the Continent to find the chalk uplands that led them with little difficulty into the interior of this country. Or they may have come across farther north, over marshes that are now the North Sea, to find the convenient chalk again in Norfolk.

The Neolithic period

The people who more definitely occupied the uplands, as distinct from wanderers and hunters, were those we call neolithic. They were pastoralists seeking grazing for their animals, but they also knew something of the arts of agriculture, and agriculture eventually demands that men should settle down on the land. They scratched fields on the slopes of the downs and sent their sheep to graze on the grass. Perhaps we must date from that time the short and springy turf that is still characteristic of the unploughed downland. The neolithic tribes built earthwork causewayed camps, the most famous of which is that on Windmill Hill, near the Overton Hill end of our

West Kennett long barrow (*Aerofilms Ltd.*)

long-distance route. A causewayed camp is a circular earthwork, the ditch of which is interrupted by unexcavated sections or causeways that give easy access to the interior; the purpose of these camps is uncertain but they do not appear to have been built for defence.

These people made pottery and wove cloth and they enjoyed a measure of tribal organisation and discipline. They were visited by traders coming from Graig Llwyd in Wales or from the Lake District to barter stone axes and fine arrowheads—a trade that suggests that already there was commercial and industrial specialisation. The tribes buried their dead, or at least the dead of their leading families, at first in wooden structures under long barrows; later the funerary chambers were built of stone, sarsen stones being conveniently at hand for the purpose. A number of these long barrows are still to be seen on the downs—there are two notable examples at East Kennett and West Kennett south of Overton Hill—the West Kennett one may be visited and entered. The famous Wayland's Smithy above Uffington on the Ridgeway is a chambered long barrow of about 2800 B.C., to which, when it was already more than three thousand years old, the name and legend of a demon smith of the Norse period became attached. Past the noble dead sleeping in the long barrow went the increasing trade of the Ridgeway.

6

Silbury Hill (*Aerofilms Ltd.*)

The Bronze Age

Somewhere, perhaps in Ireland, methods of smelting metals were discovered and ornaments of gold and weapons of copper began to form part of the stock-in-trade of merchants on the upland routes. Later, that stock-in-trade contained bronze. Itinerant smiths carried their metal with them to cast it where it was required, bartering newly made goods for old ones that could be remelted. The Ridgeway, the Icknield Way, the Harrow Way, and other such upland paths were by then distinctly trade routes.

About 1900 B.C. bronze-bearing warriors arrived in Britain. They probably made a landing first in Dorset, where they found the chalk ridge convenient for their penetration of the country. We recognise them from their custom of burying their dead with a drinking vessel, called a beaker, a custom that has given them their name of the Beaker Folk. They overcame and submerged the Windmill Hill people.

The Beaker Folk were builders, for to them must be credited the foundation of Stonehenge and of Avebury. The latter they set down only about a mile to the south of their predecessors' centre on Windmill Hill. They are probably also responsible for that mysterious mound, Silbury Hill, the purpose of which, and its date, are still unknown, despite investigations that included a widely publicised dig on behalf of the BBC in 1969.

Within a few generations the Beaker Folk of Wessex had to submit in their turn to a new incursion. Able and well-armed warriors from Brittany established a kind of aristocratic hegemony of considerable splendour. The chalk highways now saw an increase in trade, including expensive luxury goods. Jet came from Yorkshire, amber from the Baltic, gold from Ireland, and blue faience beads from as far away as Egypt. There was a growing commercial economy, and all without the benefit of money.

These Wessex aristocrats buried their dead in round barrows or tumuli of a variety of types that may be seen in large numbers on the downlands—bowl barrows like inverted saucers, bell barrows, with a flat shelf or 'berm' around a central mound, and disk barrows, like round shields with a boss at the centre. They took to the custom of cremating the bodies and putting the ashes in or under urns, from which they have been called the Urn People. Round barrows continued to be built well into Anglo-Saxon times.

The Bronze Age was interrupted in the eighth century B.C. by the arrival of a people whom for the first time we can identify with a racial name—the Celts. They came with superior weapons and superior agriculture, and with a method of growing their crops in little rectangular fields, the outlines of which are still visible in many places in air photographs of the chalk downs. More clearly visible on the ground are ditches miles long that marked the boundaries of the territories of tribes or regional chiefs. A number of these ditches are known as 'Grim's Ditch' because country people of a later date could attribute construction on such a scale only to the Devil. 'Grim' is a Norse name for Woden, whom early Christians identified with the Devil. Compare the name of the Wansdyke, which is 'Woden's ditch', and also of Grime's Graves. The longest of these Grim's Ditches runs parallel with the Ridgeway for many miles through Wiltshire, Berkshire, and Oxfordshire and seems to extend across the Thames in the form of the Grim's Ditch along which the long-distance path runs from Mongewell to Nuffield.

The Iron Age

A later wave of Celts came with iron weapons in their hands. Iron is a metal more common in the ground than tin or copper. There was iron in the ironstone of north Oxfordshire, for instance, and the Ridgeway and the Icknield Way might have been convenient for the dissemination of the product. More and more Celts landed in Britain. The earlier comers saw no reason to welcome the new arrivals as their relations—the newcomers always wanted land. The established settlers hastily threw up fortifications to defend themselves and their property, and from this time date those great earthwork forts, nearly all on hill tops, that are so notable an element of the English scene. Barbury Castle, Liddington Castle, Uffington Castle, and Segsbury Camp, with lesser forts on Pulpit Hill and on Ivinghoe Beacon, are notable along the Wessex Ridgeway and the Icknield Way. Only a short distance from the path are Alfred's Castle near Ashdown Park, Hardwell Camp at Compton Beauchamp (half a

Wayland's Smithy

mile from Uffington Castle), Blewburton Camp above Blewbury, Perborough Castle south of Compton, and a fort on Boddington Hill above Wendover.

It is a curious fact that the Ridgeway Path as it is defined today does not actually touch any of these camps, but passes at a little distance from them. The only exception is Barbury, where the long-distance path goes straight through the middle of the fort. However, if we accept the Ordnance Survey line of the Ridgeway as going down to Chiseldon, Barbury accords with the general rule. In the nature of their siting the forts lie on the edge of the scarp, while the path keeps below the skyline of the downs as seen from the plain.

When the Romans came they found the Iron Age forts capable of serious resistance, especially those that had been elaborated by multiple lines of defence and were manned by companies of expert sling-shots. After the Romans left the incoming Anglo-Saxons also found that some of the forts were held against them—the battle of Beranburgh was fought in A.D. 556 near Barbury Castle.

A notable curiosity of the Iron Age on the Ridgeway is the Uffing-ton White Horse. Its beautifully simplified design is derived from ancient British coins, which, it has been shown, were in turn derived distantly from Greek originals. The Greek image of a chariot drawn by prancing horses was copied and recopied by generations of coiners and steadily degenerated until the stylised and dismembered figure of a single horse was arrived at, eminently suited to the use to which it has been put on the down.

Probably in Bronze Age times men demolished by fire or by axe sections of the lowland forests to make additional fields, but with the advance of the Iron Age came tools that could deal more expeditiously with the trees and the subsequent clearing and cultivation of the ground. New farms and new settlements, with tracks to connect them, developed on the lower land along the spring line and the old upland tracks began to be less frequented. Under the Romans and the Anglo-Saxons the settlements became villages and the tracks became roads. You may see the effect on the modern Ordnance Survey map. Beginning from Avebury the lower road, now a surfaced highway, connects a string of villages and towns—Berwick Bassett, Winterbourne Bassett, Broad Hinton, Wroughton, Chiseldon, Wanborough, Bishopstone, Woolstone, Uffington, Kingston Lisle, Letcombe Bassett, Letcombe Regis, and so on to the Thames. East of the Thames the pattern is repeated with Watlington, Lewknor, Aston Rowant, Chinnor, Princes Risborough, Tring, and on to Ivinghoe. In places the road these villages are strung on is the Icknield Way.

The Middle Ages to modern times

Throughout the Middle Ages drovers of sheep and cattle continued to use the upland ways, probably bringing beasts from Wales for the London market—on these long journeys it was often the practice to shoe the cattle with metal soles to prevent the hooves from splitting. The introduction of turnpikes in the eighteenth century would only have confirmed the drovers in their use of the upland ways, where they would avoid tolls. The bordering hedges may date from this time, planted by farmers to keep the herds and flocks out of the fields. Because those herds and flocks were often large and required a good space for passage, the hedges had to be 30 feet or more apart.

The herds and flocks have long since gone. Today the upland ways are used by farmers driving their stock from field to field, or to bring a tractor to wherever it is required. Horse-riders use them, as also do ramblers and more casual walkers, and occasional cyclists. But for much of the time, except perhaps on a fine day at a week-end, the upland ways are lonely and quiet.

Very little of the Ridgeway, but more of the Icknield Way, has been metalled. Those sections that have become surfaced motor roads have been by-passed by the long-distance path in order to maintain a route on footpaths or bridleways. A large number of roads reach or cross the path, and three motorways cross—the M4 near Liddington Castle, the M40 coming from a deep slot through the Chiltern chalk near Stokenchurch, and the Tring by-pass, the A41(M).

Celtic figures (*Amalgamated Press*)

The chalk lands

The greater part of the route with which we are concerned in this book lies along the chalk uplands. West of the Thames the chalk is that of the Wessex Downs and east of the Thames of the Chilterns. The route runs along the summit or on the slopes of the northern and north-eastern scarp, descending in places to lower ground based on the lower chalk, the greensand, and gault clay. All these strata belong in the series classified by geologists as 'Cretaceous'. The Cretaceous period, the final period of the Secondary or Mesozoic era, began a hundred and twenty million years ago and endured for some fifty to sixty million years.

Much of Britain during that time lay under the waters of an extensive warm sea. Great river systems drained into this sea, depositing sediments that, over those immense lengths of time, became thick beds of sand or mud. These beds became consolidated to form the firm greensand and the softer impermeable gault clay. A change in conditions brought about a change in the nature of the sediments. Chalky substances began to be deposited in increasing quantities with the clay, forming the marl that farmers in recent historical times were to find valuable in the manuring and sweetening of their land. The chalk content in the deposit on the sea floor became more and more predominant until pure chalk was being laid down.

The sedimentation of the Cretaceous period continued for so long that the strata attained depths of thousands of feet. The downs we see today, though they attain a height of nearly a thousand feet above sea level, are no more than the worn-down remnants of the strata laid down in the Cretaceous period.

The origin of chalk and flint

The origin of the chalk is not altogether clear. It used to be supposed that chalk consisted entirely of the shells of minute creatures, principally foraminifera, dwelling in the Cretaceous seas, which as they died dropped in a constant drizzle to the sea floor. This theory is no longer held to be true. It *is* true that part of the chalk is made up of such shells, which may be seen under a microscope. They are mixed with a more amorphous material that may be derived from the disintegration of planktonic algae. It is asserted that part of the chalk may be the result of chemical processes.

Another mysterious substance found in the chalk is flint. Flint is found in the upper chalk—the purer chalk—commonly in horizontal beds, as you may see in such chalk cliffs as Beachy Head. Flint is

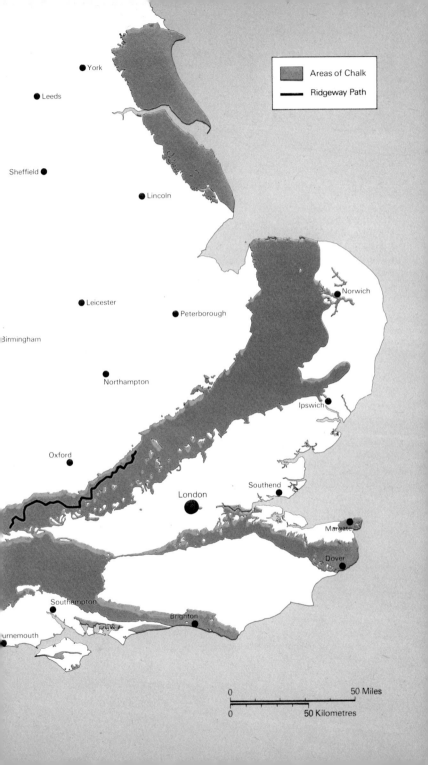

Areas of Chalk

Ridgeway Path

York

Leeds

Sheffield

Lincoln

Leicester

Peterborough

Birmingham

Northampton

Norwich

Ipswich

Oxford

London

Southend

Margate

Dover

Southampton

Brighton

urnemouth

| 0 | | | 50 Miles |

| 0 | | | 50 Kilometres |

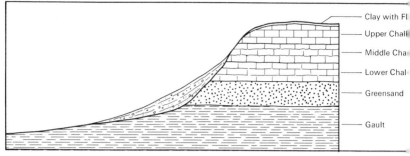

Clay with Flints
Upper Chalk
Middle Chalk
Lower Chalk
Greensand
Gault

Section of the chalk escarpment in north Wiltshire

silica and is so hard that primitive man seized upon it for his tools and weapons. Yet it was once liquid, as may be perceived in the manner in which it has flowed round remnants of various creatures and plants as fossils. It may have originated in the siliceous spicules or skeletons of sponges and other sea creatures, which dissolved, the solution flowing where it could, probably into small cavities in the chalk. Why such cavities should have existed, and in such large numbers and in such curious shapes, needs explanation.

The chalk deposits ceased, but other sediments continued to form and clays and sands were deposited on top of the chalk.

The Alpine storm

The Cretaceous period closed with earth tremors and uplifts of the land. These increased in intensity and became the enormous cataclysms of what geologists call 'the Alpine storm'. This storm of earthquakes and earth movements raised up the Alps as its greatest monument in Europe. It altered the sea levels everywhere and pushed and bent and fractured the strata and heaved them up in folds as high hills and mountains. The level sediments of the Cretaceous period rose from the sea as mountains. No sooner did they appear than the sub-aerial demolition teams of wind, rain, frost, and ice began their patient and destructive work. These destroyers slowly stripped off the overlying strata down to the more resistant chalk— chalk is resistant because it is permeable and rain passes through it. When the rain is acid, however, it dissolves the chalk, and to this effect the smoothness of the contours of the chalk uplands is attributable.

Because the chalk is permeable rivers do not form on the surface. You will look in vain for springs and wells in the chalk that would be the birthplaces of rivers. But look along the lower contours and you will find springs and wells rising where the chalk lies on impermeable clay or perhaps on a stratum of harder chalk rock. Men have made use of this reservoir under the chalk in modern times by sinking boreholes into it.

Yet experience on the ground and examination of the contours on the map reveal valleys in the upland chalk that are evidently the valleys of streams, from which the streams have long since disappeared. These valleys may have been formed when the whole

14

water-table was higher and rain water remained on the surface long enough to flow off as streams; or perhaps when the ground was frozen, with the same effect. Down such a valley, Temple Bottom, goes the track from the Ridgeway to Temple Farm and Rockley, and down another, and confluent, the road from Broad Hinton to Marlborough. There are further examples on each side of the Ridgeway where it drops down to Streatley, and again in the repeated folds of the Chilterns that converge on Chesham.

Remnants of former strata

As the sediments above the chalk dissolved they left behind their insoluble constituents. These lie on the chalk principally as a layer called 'clay-with-flints' — in some places it is rather clay with pebbles. This forms the 'earth' of the chalk-hill farmer, on which his grass grows and which he ploughs for his crops. The number of flints is incredible, as you may see on many a ploughed field, which may appear white from the thick salting of chalk- or lime-covered flints.

Another remnant of the strata that overlay the chalk is the sarsen stone. The stones are sometimes called 'grey wethers' from their fancied resemblance to resting sheep. The stones are hard lumps formed in sandstone and left behind when the softer sandstone was eroded away. Many of these stones are very large—as for example the portal stones of the West Kennett long barrow and the stones that form the circles of Avebury. Through the centuries farmers have rooted sarsens out of the ploughlands, but there are places where they still occur in large numbers. On the 2½-inch map the area of Fyfield Down, west of the Ridgeway near Overton Hill, is speckled with indications of sarsens, and there they may be seen on the ground; there are said to be 25,000 of them. Numbers of them line the Ridgeway itself from Overton Hill northwards.

The geological and geomorphological picture of the land east of the Ridgeway is more complex. The scarp is more indented, giving rise to what appear as individual hills, such as Lodge Hill, Coombe Hill, and the Beacon hills. The scarp remains at an altitude of about 700 feet, but it would be a tiresome up-and-down or back-and-forth path that followed it. Here both the ancient highways and the long-distance path run frequently at a lower altitude, about 300 or 400 feet.

1 and 2 Bronze Age axe-heads. 3 and 4 Bronze Age funerary pottery. 5 Sickle from first millennium B.C. (*With acknowledgements to the Royal Archaeological Institute*)

Flora and fauna

Wild flowers

Many kinds of plants grow in the various environments of the long-distance footpath. This chapter cannot pretend to mention more than a selection of those that are common, together with a few that are more or less rare.

Broadly, three classes of plants will be found along the Ridgeway Path. The first comprises those plants that characteristically grow and flourish on chalk and do not do well elsewhere; these are *calcicole* plants. When, for example, you see traveller's joy (old man's beard) you will know that you must be on chalk. The second class includes those plants that are less particular and which will flourish on many kinds of soil. The third class is the acid-loving or chalk-hating (*calcifuge*) plants; these you will find only where the chalk is covered with an acid layer of clay-with-flints, as on Fyfield Down or Coombe Hill. Calcifuge plants include heather, ling, and gorse.

Most of the fields along the path are under the plough. Poppies may be seen in the corn, but not in anything like the numbers that used to be common. Wild plants in this cultivated terrain are likely to be few and those mostly annuals. You should look for other plants, indeed for a variety of plants in general, on ground that has seldom been ploughed or on ground that has never been ploughed at all. Some of the downland has not been under cultivation since neolithic times. It has, however, been grazed by sheep or cattle or both, and as a result has developed a low-lying herbage or sward that may contain a surprising variety of dwarfed plants. Perhaps grazing has been the cause of the evolution of the stemless thistle, whose flowers and large rosettes of leaves cling close to the ground. On the other hand, ragwort seems to have solved the problem of survival by being unpalatable and it is therefore able to lift its yellow flowers a foot or eighteen inches into the air.

There are other kinds of land that are not cultivated and which may be found to be the home of interesting plants. Tumuli and barrows, where they still exist, have been left alone by the plough-man, and, in cornland, kept safe from grazing animals. Iron Age forts and many other earthworks share the same immunity from the plough, but are subject to grazing—incidentally, do not expect to find visible earthworks on the ground wherever they are marked on the map—many have been ploughed down and may be recognised only from the air.

The richest, the most luxuriant, the most varied in their flora, and the most obvious places are the broad verges of the long-distance path. The wide and lordly Wessex Ridgeway and similar stretches along the Icknield track are worn by use, for the greater part, only in the middle, where farm tractors and Land-Rovers mark out a double line. The rest is wild land thick in spring and summer with many kinds of grasses and flowering plants, and overhung in places by a variety of bushes and trees.

In spring the accent among the flowers is on white and yellow. The white blossoms of the sloe or blackthorn shine early on the bare black twigs, and later come the more profuse blossoms of the hawthorn and the elder. Crab-apples display white blossom tinged with pink. Dogwood and the wayfaring tree also add white to the hedgerows, with the whitebeam lifting it to a higher level. Among the grass wild candytuft, white with pink, will be found, with hogweed and wild carrot spreading their white umbels. Beneath these, and especially along the edges of ruts and of ploughed fields, the scentless mayweed opens its daisy-like flowers. Apparently liking to be crushed underfoot, the rayless chamomile or pineapple mayweed forms a green and sulphur-yellow carpet where the passage of feet is frequent.

As the season advances the yellows become more numerous. The rock-rose may not be found often, but it is certainly a plant of the chalk. Ragwort is ubiquitous from June onwards. The little yellow pea-flowers of the melilot and of dyers' greenweed climb in spikes, neat when compared with the loose, untidy yellow heads of lady's bedstraw. Low down, the orange to red flowers of the bird's-foot trefoil burn in the grass. Crowds of hawkbits raise their yellow heads to the light with flowers that look like dandelions with the petal ends notched or cut square.

In June and July the verges become a palette of yellows and purples. The yellow umbels of wild parsley rise above the neighbouring herbage, profuse in places. Wild mignonette is common too, but it has no scent. Among the purples the cranesbills and brush-like heads of knapweed make the principal chord—the latter are beautiful flowers with an unfortunate name. Nearly as frequent are the lilac to pink varieties of scabious. There are many purple thistles, some of which grow strongly on grazed ground, avoided by both sheep and cattle. You may, too, come upon the yellow carline thistle, distinguished by the shape of its flowers and its colour. Marjoram grows in colonies, with heads of purple flowers, and wild basil, too, is purple; both are relatives of the garden varieties. The clustered bellflower and the nettle-leaved bellflower blossom from June onwards. Another bell-shaped flower, the autumn gentian, may be found later, but it is not very common.

Between June and August, and often later, several varieties of orchid may be found on the chalk. The pyramid orchid and the fragrant orchid are similar in appearance, but the latter smells of carnations. The flower of the bee orchid looks quite realistically as though a large bee were sucking honey from among the petals—its identity cannot be mistaken. Botanists have learned by bitter experience not to advertise the sites of unusual flowers, and if you find such flowers you will do well to be equally reticent. But perhaps not if you find the extremely rare military orchid, whose flower resembles

18 a little man wearing an enormous helmet. Don't tell the newspapers

about the scene of your triumph; instead tell a responsible botanical society. Any of these orchids, with others, may be found in the Chilterns, where also you may come upon the Chiltern gentian, very like, but larger than, the autumn gentian.

Harebells are by no means rare, but you are unlikely to find them in large numbers. Near trees or high hedges grow cohorts of rosebay willowherb, up to six feet high. Yellow toadflax and mullein seem to be as much at home near trees as they are in more open ground. White bryony twines over the hedges, together with field bindweed, the latter with small pink trumpets rayed with white. Sweet alison grows on Lodge Hill, perhaps an escape from some distant garden.

Many kinds of trees grow on the chalk. Elm, ash, oak, lime, sycamore, field maple, and juniper will all be found, together with various introduced conifers in small plantations. There are horse-chestnuts too. The Chilterns are famous for their beechwoods, and no tree is more handsome or more attractive, especially when the fringed young leaves of spring are fresh and translucent on the bough. Here and there you will find an aspen, which in August may advertise itself by littering the ground beneath, and the branches of the neighbouring trees, with its white and fluffy catkins, like so much teased cotton wool.

Birds

The birds to be seen or heard along the path include most of those common to the southern half of England, for there is sufficient variety of environment to suit them. The lark and the meadow pipit are heard above the downland, the latter ending its song suddenly to drop like a stone into the grass. Earlier or later in the year lapwings (plovers) gather and call 'peewit, peewit', and the linnet sings from the stubble. In the hedges live yellowhammers, dunnocks, blackbirds, thrushes, chaffinches, robins, and wrens. Pheasants and partridges are also birds of the open country, together with wheatears in summer and fieldfares in winter. Corncrakes turn their rusty hinges in the summer corn, and the nightjar may still be heard. Wood-pigeons and collared doves burble in the taller hedges and in the trees. In the woods the machine-gun fire of woodpeckers is always startling. Tree-creepers may be seen in the woods and on beeches bramblings. Nightingales sing in the lower areas. Sparrowhawks prey in the woodlands and over the more open country kestrels plane with pointed wings.

Animals

With luck you may see a fox. He preys on the numerous rabbits along the length of the track and leaves behind the shredded and scattered fur. In more open country he finds hares. Especially in the evening you are likely to see a hare ahead of you on the track, standing quite still with head and ears erect until he is sure you are coming his way, when he is off with a bound. At harvest time hares and rabbits flee bewildered from the square of corn diminishing as the combines work. There are badgers in plenty but the only evidence of their presence you are likely to see is their massive excavations—nothing else is capable of the digging the badger does. Field-mice and shrews 19 scuttle in the deep grass, while in the corn you may find the climbing harvest mouse or its suspended nest. In Tring Park and in the neighbouring Chilterns lives the edible dormouse, introduced into the park from the Continent in 1902. The grey squirrel is common wherever there are trees, the red squirrel unfortunately not.

Racehorses are a frequent sight in the neighbourhood of Lambourn and the Ilsleys. Most of the cattle in the pastures are black and white. They share the grazing with herds of sheep. A flock of unusual sheep parti-coloured brown and white inhabits Coombe Hill above Ellesborough.

There are probably snakes along the path, for the conditions appear to be suitable for them—if not perhaps for adders then surely for grass-snakes, but I have not seen a single example. Nor have I seen lizards or slow-worms, though I would expect them to be present. Perhaps my footfall is too heavy and they disappear into hiding.

Insects

The usual wide spectrum of varieties may be found along the paths. In summer fat damp flies are a pest in leafy lanes and woodlands. There are occasional biting horseflies. A large variety of spiders spread their nets and traps. Beetles of many kinds crawl among the herbage, including the fearsome but harmless stag-beetle. It is the butterflies that are the most interesting and attractive, from the milk chocolate meadow brown to the colourful peacock and the tortoiseshells. The elegant marbled white will be seen, and also the fritillaries. The chalkhill blue is reputedly rare, but not too rare to be encountered perhaps several times in the course of 85 miles.

Opposite (left): Pyramidal orchid; (centre): Military or soldier orchid; (right): Bee orchid

How to do it

The long-distance path is primarily a footpath and the most satis-
factory method of exploring it is to walk it. Indeed, for nearly half of
the way your two feet will provide the only convenient means of
progress as well as the one for which you have any legal right of way
throughout. Along much of the route not only is the ground too rough
for the comfortable use of a vehicle, but there is the hindrance of
stiles.

The path may be walked in short stretches from road-head to
road-head or road crossing, the longest such stretch being about
five and a half miles from the A34 above East Ilsley to the lower
Warren Farm at the foot of Thurle Down west of Streatley. Or it may
be tackled in longer stretches—since there are no hindering crags
or high, steep hills to impede progress—by strong walkers capable
of twenty miles or more in a day.

Along much of the Icknield track and nearly all of the Wessex
upland way there is scope for overnight camping, and many walkers
carry a small tent for this purpose. In making your plans, however,
you must keep in mind the fact that visits to neighbouring villages
for supplies will add two to four miles to the day's total, with the
return to the Ridgeway an uphill trudge.

Campers will find water supply a problem. There are no wells or
springs on the uplands, and along the Wessex upland way there are
few farms at which to ask for water. That people do ask at those few
farms, and that farmers frequently interrupted by such demands may
be understandably tetchy, may be deduced from the bold sign at one
place, 'No water available here'. You may be well advised to obtain
water in the villages where you buy your supplies.

If you are camping make your load as light as you possibly can.
Reject everything that is not absolutely essential. There is no fun
and no sense in carrying fifty or sixty pounds on your back, for with
such a weight, even if you have the strength to walk far, your feet
may not stand the strain. A wise young man we met at Ivinghoe was
carrying a very light pack with a tent and proposed to cover the
eighty-five miles in four and a half days. Two teen-age girls at
Wendover, on the other hand, had packs so heavy they had difficulty
in lifting them—these two certainly would not go far, nor would they
be happy in their journey.

A family of five we encountered near Overton Hill emulated

Robert Louis Stevenson by carrying all their supplies and equipment on a donkey, putting up their tent wherever they arrived for the night. It is an excellent idea (if you can get a donkey) and practicable on the Wessex upland way, but not on the Icknield track (see Horse-riding below) because of the stiles there. The disadvantage would be that you would be restricted to the pace of the animal. And of course you would have to make provision for returning it at the end of the journey.

Horse-riding

Near Lambourn and East Ilsley the Ridgeway passes through very horsey country and you will see beside the way long lengths of turfed ground used as private gallops, and fields with fences for steeplechase training. The whole length of the Wessex Ridgeway from Overton Hill to Streatley is open to horse-riders, but for miles ruts will restrict progress to a walk. East of the Thames the Icknield track is really suitable only for short hacks. Riders who propose to make long-distance treks will find no lack of grass for feed, but they should take account of the lack of water and of accommodation for horse and man. They should also be provided with the addresses and telephone numbers of local veterinary surgeons and farriers in case of emergency.

East of the Thames the picture is more mixed, with lengths of footpath alternating with lengths of bridleway.

The following list gives the stretches of the long-distance path open to horse-riders:

Overton Hill to Goring (along Smeathe's Ridge); about 45 miles.

From North Stoke to Mongewell; 1¼ miles.

From the A4074 at Mongewell along Grim's Ditch for approximately 1¼ miles—difficult because of close-growing trees and bushes.

A fragment in Swyncombe Park, past Swyncombe church to the surfaced road.

Along the Icknield Way from a point near North Farm south of Britwell to a point south of Bledlow; about 9 miles.

A short distance on the east slope of Lodge Hill.

About 1 mile from the A4010 south of Princes Risborough.

About 1 mile from the road junction south of Chequers to Lodge Hill.

About 1 mile from Wendover church to Boswell's Farm.

Cycling

Only a determined cyclist would want to lift his machine over the many high stiles of the Icknield track and push it through the deep mould of the woods. I would deter any cyclist from attempting the Icknield half of the long-distance path—in any case, except for a few short stretches, it is not legally open to cyclists.

The Wessex upland way is mostly wide lane with no great rise or fall of the land, but the surface in most places is deeply furrowed. Some stretches, in summer, are thick with long grass, which will encumber the wheels. Along the path in general there will be a good deal of pushing to be done.

C

Motor-cycling

Motor-cyclists have no right on the greater part of the long-distance path. In general the surface is rough and treacherous even for would-be rough-riders, and indeed is dangerous.

Motor-cars

Various interests, including the Ramblers' Association, are seeking to exclude power-driven wheeled vehicles from the long-distance path—rightly so. A walker or a cyclist does no harm to anybody and does not detract in his use of the path from the enjoyment of that use by others. Any powered vehicle pollutes the air, damages the track, and brings noise and discomfort to other users. In fact, in the present state of the track anyone who attempts to drive along the Ridgeway can have little concern for his car or his pocket, nor a realisation of the probable high expense of recovering a broken-down vehicle from any part of the path distant from a road.

The most useful employment of a car is as a mobile centre from which sections of the path may be walked. True, this means walking a distance and then having to come back to the car again, so that in effect you walk the path twice. This is what my wife and I have done, completing the double journey in a fortnight, with an average of rather more than twelve miles a day. Easy going, but we were there to observe and to note.

There is some parking space, for from a few to many cars, at nearly every point where a surfaced road meets or crosses the long-distance path. The principal restrictions or prohibition of parking will be found in the neighbourhood of the Prime Minister's house at Chequers.

Warning

Because all parts of the long-distance path are easily reached from London and such urban centres as Reading, Oxford, Swindon, etc., it is subject to thieves. Tents left untenanted are a temptation, but a greater temptation is parked cars. Cars may be parked for hours while the occupants go off to explore, and thieves have plenty of time to get in, grab their booty, and leave. This warning has a personal basis, for such a thief broke into my car, smashing the lock, and made off with my wife's handbag (which had been concealed). Perhaps there is no sure way of keeping these gentry out—they may have so much available time that possibly not even a car burglar alarm would deter them. The only answer is not to leave valuables, especially money, in your car. If a group of hefty hikers were to catch these fellows in the act, and express their strong indignation, the sequel might be illegal but it would be satisfying.

Equipment

The long-distance path passes over country neither high nor severe. Almost all of the land over which it goes is agricultural, producing cereals—oats, wheat, and large quantities of barley. This is an indication of the geniality of the climate, in spring and summer at
24 least. Many fields are given over to grazing, either of sheep or of

cattle—often black and white Friesians. The picture is one of temperate conditions. Yet in wet weather, or in a cool or cold season, the uplands of the long-distance path may be bleak and consequently little frequented. Therefore if you are going to walk it in such a season you should treat the upland as you would more mountainous country and should prepare for some of the eventualities of that kind of country.

Nevertheless, the special costume adopted by mountain walkers as on the Pennine Way or the Cleveland Way, designed to protect the wearer from extreme conditions, is not essential in any but bad weather. During much of the year you could walk the Ridgeway long-distance path in a lounge suit if you really wished to. In bad weather some elements of mountain-walking costume are advisable. A hooded anorak or parka, or a cagoule, will be comfortable and comforting, and a spare pullover will help to guard against chill. Strong and comfortable shoes that are old enough to fit well are essential in any weather. The soles should preferably be of the vibram or Itshide pattern—smooth soles will slip on the clay and on the chalk if it is wet, and thin ones will allow flints and pebbles to make a sharp and painful impression. Boots, rather than shoes, may be desirable in wet weather, when both the chalk and the clay of the path become heavy and sticky and the loam of the woods soft and clinging. In summer wear two pairs of thin socks for distance walking, rather than one thicker pair, and in winter two thick pairs. These will cushion your feet and help to prevent blisters. Just in case, despite the socks, you do get blisters, carry half a dozen 'Band-Aid' plasters. Also carry a crêpe bandage in case a foot is twisted or sprained on the ruts.

A compass may be essential on mountain tracks, but it is not *necessary* on the Ridgeway long-distance path. The route is made plain by its character and by waymarking. However, a compass will be useful, in conjunction with the map, to identify features in the extensive views that are obtained from many parts of the path.

If you lose your way despite the marking of the path, you will not be lost in any mountaineering sense. Wherever you may be you will not be far from habitation and within a short distance you will find a path or a road descending to a farm or a village. Mist sometimes clouds the downs, but it is not the danger that it can be in the mountains; while, of course, there are steep slopes on the down sides, especially in the neighbourhood of the White Horse at Uffington, there are no crags or precipices. Nevertheless, it is possible to be incapacitated by an accident or sudden illness, and in case of this carry a whistle, or at night a flashlight, with which you can give the recognised trouble signal.

Maps

The 2½-inch maps in this book give excellent information about the long-distance path itself and its immediate neighbourhood, but they are restricted in their coverage of the areas seen in the extensive views. The new 1:50,000 (1¼-inch) Ordnance Survey maps complement the 2½-inch maps in this respect. Sheets 173, 174, 175, and 165 cover the whole length of the path from Overton Hill to Ivinghoe Beacon.

Note

In the itinerary I have referred to cornfields in the sense of fields sown to any kind of cereal. Fields I found growing corn may be sown with grass or lucerne, or beans or maize, next year, and readers should allow for such possible changes.

Though the long-distance path, especially along the Chilterns, often lies north-east to south-west, and sometimes due north or due south, I have for the sake of simplicity referred to 'east-bound' and 'west-bound' travellers. This book describes the journey from west to east. Where I have found parts of the course likely to give difficulty to west-bound travellers I have inserted an elucidation of the route for their benefit; these bits are printed in italics.

Overton Hill to Ogbourne St. George

about 10 miles

The traveller setting foot on the Ridgeway at Overton Hill will be conscious that he is on a very ancient highway. He has only to turn his head to find a group of six round barrows beside the path, in the corner formed by the Bath road—the Roman road to Bath passed through the central gap of these barrows and crossed the Ridgeway. In a field next to the far side of the modern road, beside the lay-by where our traveller may park his car, he will see the markers of the stone circle called, since Stukeley gave it that name in the eighteenth century, the Sanctuary. He may see, too, on the hills to the south the tree-covered mound of the East Kennett long barrow and to the south-west the West Kennett long barrow. Within a mile is the vast stone circle of Avebury, and south of it, beside the Bath road, the enigmatic mound of Silbury Hill. Each of these may be four thousand years old, and perhaps older.

The East Kennett long barrow lies on the hillside south of the river Kennett and the pleasant little village of East Kennett. The barrow is on private land and there is no right of way to it, but you may recognise it by its covering of tall trees. It has not been excavated. Every archaeologist would dearly like the chance to open this barrow and to find its perhaps untouched treasures—not gold or jewels but bones, with pottery and implements that might add to our knowledge of the people who built the long barrows.

The West Kennett long barrow *has* been opened and it may be visited. It is reached in half a mile by a footpath starting from the A4 within a few yards of Silbury Hill. The hill, the largest artificial mound in Europe, is of unknown date and unknown purpose. It is so large that Stonehenge would fit on its flat top. The West Kennett long barrow was built about 2500 B.C., and its five stone-lined chambers were used over the following thousand years for the burial of not fewer than forty-six persons of all ages; the remains of these people were found in an excavation done in 1955–56. The barrow is 330 ft. long, 80 ft. wide, and 10 ft. high. It was originally flanked by ditches 12 ft. deep, from which the material of the barrow was taken, but these have long since silted up. The stones of the forecourt are enormous sarsens.

Avebury is world-famous and it is not unusual to hear half a dozen languages, from Japanese to German, spoken by visitors wandering 27

Ridgeway signpost

Top (opposite): Norman font at Avebury

Below (opposite): Earthwork near Avebury (*Aerofilms Ltd.*)

among the great standing stones. The huge stone circle, the largest
of its kind—more than a dozen times larger than Stonehenge—with
lesser circles within it, is contained within a ditch and bank. This
ditch and bank earthwork originally measured 55 ft. from top to
base and it is still impressive. When John Aubrey came here in the
early seventeenth century the monument was practically complete,
but when William Stukeley arrived a hundred years later damage
by farmers had begun.

No explanation of so large a monument other than that it was a
temple seems possible—a cathedral of a religion of which we have
long since lost the object and the relevance.

In the Middle Ages a village grew up partly within the circle and
partly outside. Its church of St. James was built *outside* the circle,
no doubt to avoid the influence of the pagan stones. Originally
Anglo-Saxon and Norman, the church has later alterations and a
fifteenth-century west tower. It contains an ornate Norman font
and a splendid, if restored, Perpendicular rood screen.

Near the tower a small National Trust museum relates to the
28 Avebury circle, and behind this stands Avebury Manor, built about

West Kennett long barrow with large standing stones at the entrance

1557 on the site of a Benedictine monastic foundation. The house and gardens are open to visitors.

An avenue of standing stones led from Avebury to the Sanctuary on Overton Hill. Some of these stones remain beside the B4003.

We should know nothing of the Sanctuary if it were not for Stukeley, who saw it standing. It was destroyed in the seventeenth century to make way for the plough. Excavation has revealed the sites of stone-holes and post-holes, and these suggest that the circle as it originally stood enclosed a round wooden hut.

The Ridgeway leaves Overton Hill due north as an unmistakable track, broad and free and climbing gently over downland partly ploughed for corn and partly under grass. Occasional sarsen stones line the path, and there are tumuli more or less distant. Within a few yards of the Ridgeway café there was once a stone circle, but nothing is to be seen of it now. At a crossing of paths that on the west goes down to Avebury, that on the east goes over Overton Down to Fyfield Down. The Ordnance Survey marks this eastward path 'herepath'. Old English *here* meant 'army' or a 'multitude' and *here-*

path meant a track wide enough for an army or a multitude of people to move on. The word is applied also to certain lengths of the Ridgeway.

There are numerous sarsen stones scattered on Overton Down and Fyfield Down and no doubt for that reason this land has escaped the plough. The stones blend into the landscape and are not easy to make out from a distance but you may walk here on footpaths to see them for yourself. There are also ancient field systems, which appear as low banks enclosing square or rectangular areas. A mound that shines white in the sun is an experimental long barrow raised in 1965. It shows how time deals with these structures. Even in so short a period as ten years the accompanying ditches have begun to silt up and the chalk mound to be seeded by plants—on genuine long barrows the flanking ditches have filled up so much that they may no longer be visible. The white chalk of the experimental mound, however, still shows clearly and this leads the observer to realise that the many long and round barrows on the chalk downs must have been decidedly eye-catching, probably through several centuries. 31

Towards Hackpen Hill

Though it is used by the landowner for grazing and there are notable racehorse training gallops, Fyfield Down is a nature reserve of the Nature Conservancy Council. Here hares, rabbits, voles, and various mice live and are prey for foxes, badgers, weasels and stoats, as well as for long- and short-eared owls, buzzards, sparrowhawks, and kestrels.

The track takes a sharp right turn and in a few yards turns as sharply left at a junction of paths, one of which goes down the flank of Rough Hill into Temple Bottom and to the hamlet of Rockley and the other back to Clatford Down. The Ridgeway continues northwest and then north, soon to climb on a broad way towards a prominent shaggy barrow and the ridge of Hackpen Hill, which has its name from Old English *haca*, hook-shaped. You will notice that hereabouts you walk for a time not on firm chalk but on soft earth or clay littered with flints.

At the crossing with the surfaced Broad Hinton road there is room to park several cars.

Below the crossing the road describes a broad hairpin round a hill-

On Hackpen Hill. On the horizon is a barrow

side on which is the figure of a white horse cut in 1838. It cannot be seen from the Ridgeway itself, but a hill figure always suggests a broad panorama and there is one here, over a plain from which rises the inconsiderable knob of Windmill Hill, the site of a well-known neolithic causewayed camp. On the plain lie the villages of the Winterbournes and Broad Hinton.

The broad track, rutted and grass-grown, continues north past two mixed spinneys that assume the bun-shape characteristic of the blustered downland clumps. The ground under the more southerly one is irregular, as though it were an earthwork. There are other earthworks marked on the map about here, but for most of the year they lie under the corn.

As the track descends we come to a distant view of the strong entrenchments of Barbury Castle, which takes its name from an Anglo-Saxon chief called Bera. According to the Anglo-Saxon Chronicle, he fought a battle in A.D. 556 on the slopes north of the castle, where there are traces of earthworks. The western slopes of the castle are interesting for the outlines of banks one may see there, 33 including a rectangular enclosure that may be part of a settlement older than the castle. Barbury is multivallate with entrances east and west.

As you approach the castle you walk over myriads of flints. Perhaps here, near an ancient settlement and an ancient defensive earthwork, is a good place to look for worked flints, though, of course, Barbury Castle is of the Iron Age.

Before the castle we come to a surfaced road coming up from Wroughton and beyond this a grassy track continues along the lower slope of Barbury Hill. This lower track, according to the Ordnance Survey and other authorities, is the Ridgeway, going down to Chiseldon, where it becomes surfaced. The long-distance footpath avoids this surfaced stretch by turning south, up the road, to a gate and a path that leads directly through the castle by the original entrance and exit. As you puff up the hill think of those who intended to attack the castle and, breathless, were inhospitably received by the defenders. The interior is a clear plain of $11\frac{1}{2}$ acres, with a sense of enclosure. Beyond the east side the track passes over a ditch and bank, an outwork of the castle, and along a field to a gate, which gives access to a sharp contrast, a large gravelled car park. This has a ladies' and gents' and also a wooden building on the outer walls of which are displayed leaflets, maps, and photographs, some of which are in memory of Richard Jefferies and of Alfred Williams, the latter a labourer who wrote attractive poems and essays. Each of them loved and often visited this area, from here to Liddington Castle.

At the end of the car park the path dives through a length of narrow, hedged lane, to come out on to a concrete road beside modern farm buildings. We go straight ahead and beyond the buildings find a Ridgeway signpost on the right pointing across the road to a gate and a stile on the left. The track continuing straight ahead, past clumps of trees, leads over a ridge of Marlborough Downs and into Marlborough. It looks inviting and as though it ought to be the Ridgeway itself. We pass over the stile into a cornfield with a weedy round barrow on our left. The path through the corn is broad and clear and it leads over Smeathe's Ridge, one of the most pleasant parts of the long-distance path. 'Smeathe', of course, is another form of the familiar 'Smith' or 'Smythe'. Smeathe's Ridge, rising to 690 ft., is truly a ridge of the chalk, with rounded hill slopes falling away on each side, on the south side in a steep valley that goes down to the farm of Upper Poughcombe, on the north down to the derelict red-brick buildings of the Ogbourne St. George military camp. We descend past old thorn trees into a rough lane, which passes the tail end of the camp and joins a metalled road. We follow this road south for a few yards until it turns sharply left. Our path goes straight ahead as an unsurfaced lane between bushes and trees.

Ogbourne St. George is named from an Anglo-Saxon Occa and his stream and the dedication of its thirteenth-century to fifteenth-century church is, of course, to Saint George. The church contains a good brass of Thomas Goddard, d. 1517, and his wife. Near the church is the manor-house, dated 1619.

Barbury Castle (*Aerofilms Ltd.*)

Avebury

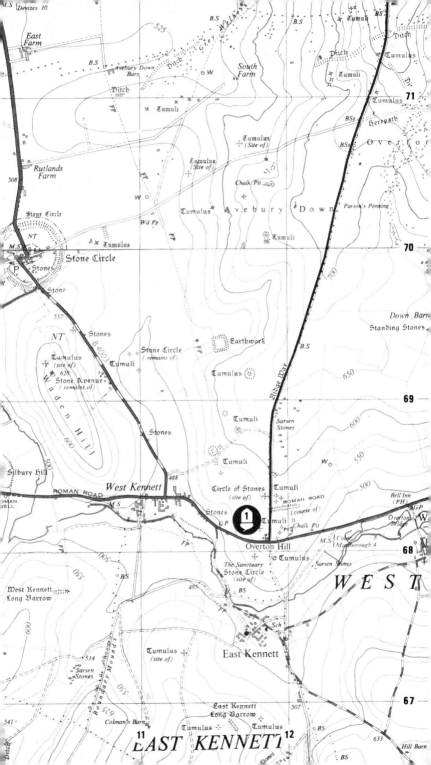

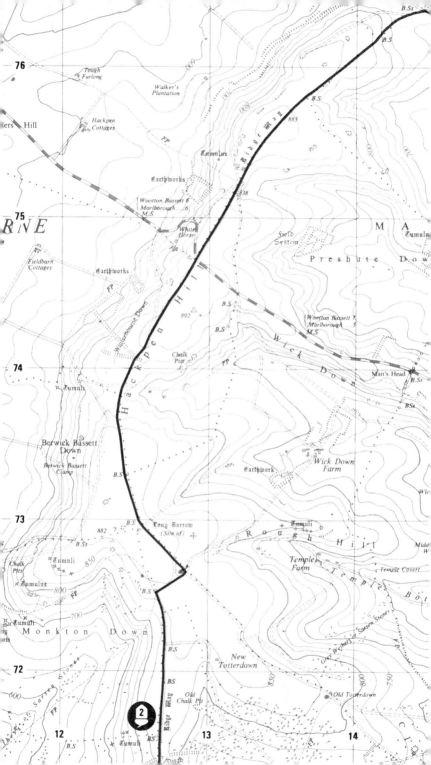

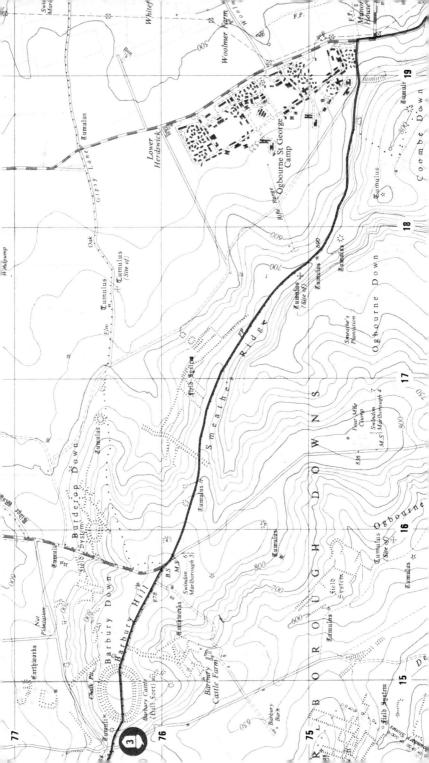

Ogbourne St. George to Uffington Castle

about 12 miles

The tree-lined lane from the military camp at Ogbourne St. George keeps for about three-quarters of a mile to the 600-ft. contour of Coombe Down. It then descends and crosses a little bridge over the reed-filled stream of the modest river Og into the hamlet of Southend, a pleasant and varied cluster of old houses. Some of the houses are timber-framed and thatched—but do not be deceived by some modern imitations. The village has a general air of prosperity and of order that suggests that most of the cottages are not now the homes of poor artisans and farm labourers as they once were.

The curving street along which the cottages lie comes out on to the A345. We cross this to enter a lane on the far side. The lane rises between trees and bushes and the abutments of a former bridge. At about 600 ft. it crosses a Roman road, now a surfaced lane coming up from Ogbourne St. George. Close against the north-east corner of the crossing is an earthwork that appears to be part of an Iron Age camp or fort, but it is not marked as such on the 2½-inch map. Overhung by bushes, the track continues north to another crossing, where the Old Chase Road comes up the scarp past a chalk-pit. The track turning east from here passes over a long linear earthwork in Yielding Copse to join the surfaced Stock Lane running past Lewisham Castle and on to Aldbourne. The castle, two miles from the Ridgeway Path, is a motte and bailey earthwork, perhaps raised by Louis the Dauphin (later Louis VIII) during his attempt in 1215–16 to claim the English throne from King John.

As it climbs north on to Round Hill Down the Ridgeway Path becomes overgrown, though still a lane, until it joins a surfaced road coming from Cowcroft Farm. This takes us to the crossing of Copse Drove from Ogbourne St. George, a surfaced road going to Aldbourne. There is space here to park two or three cars. Round Hill and the neighbouring Whitefield Hill are covered with linear ditch earthworks and field systems, nearly all on the western slope. The traveller on the Ridgeway Path, however, sees nothing of them.

North of the Copse Drove crossing, the track runs beside a field and then enters a dank lane, which goes, for about a mile, between hawthorn, blackthorn, and elderberry bushes, and various trees, with some honeysuckle and wild roses. In warm weather this lane is pestered with flies. Half-way along it a war-time strongpoint hides in an overgrown corner—a curious place to expect the Germans, you may suppose, until you remember the nearness of the military 41

'Herepath' near Liddington Castle

Top (opposite): Overgrown section above Bishopstone, Liddington Castle on the skyline

Below (opposite): Liddington Castle (*Aerofilms Ltd.*)

camps at Chiseldon and Ogbourne St. George, and of the airfield at Wroughton.

We come out into the open air with relief, at a junction of tracks. That to the west descends to Lower Upham Farm, through a linear earthwork that is clearly seen. The track to the east goes to Upper Upham, a hamlet set among so many remnant earthworks and field systems that it may not be unreasonable to suppose that there have been people living here continuously since the Iron Age, and perhaps as far back as the Bronze Age. Upper Upham may well claim to be one of the oldest settlements in England. The track past it goes on to Aldbourne, passing a line of three barrows, one of which is known as the Giant's Grave.

A Ridgeway signpost shows the direction of our track. It is straight ahead, through a gate into a field. The track becomes a mere path, not yet defined by use, round the edge of the field beneath old thorn trees and then beneath a brief row of mature beeches. The next mile runs in the open along the margins of several wide-spreading corn-fields, a path knobbly underfoot and in summer thick with long grass and errant corn. It is none the less a pleasant walk, with extensive views to the west and down an occasional combe to the east. Far in

the west the Cotswolds sprawl mistily along the horizon. To the east you may have glimpses, along Shipley Bottom, of Sugar Hill, whose modest scarp, lower than the land on which we stand, extends from Liddington to Aldbourne; along this ridge there are several barrows.

For the last part of the route towards Liddington Castle the path is called, on the OS map, a 'herepath', but any suggestion of a track broad enough to take a host is no longer evident; instead, modern travellers walk in single file. Also on the map, but not very evident on the ground, at least for the traveller on the Ridgeway Path, are extensive ditches, which appear to continue from those of Whitefield Hill to curl with the contour and join Liddington Castle. Were these additional defences for the castle, or merely boundary lines? The characteristic notched silhouette of a hill-fort shows exactly where the castle is, on the edge of the scarp, with a thin clump of trees on a nearby hill to emphasise it. The castle consists of an enclosing bank and ditch and a counterscarp bank. It is of the Iron Age, but a number of finds of post-Roman objects suggest that this defensive work was in use and perhaps inhabited into Anglo-Saxon times.

True to form the Ridgeway Path does not touch the castle and you must turn aside if you wish to visit it. Below the castle lie the village of Liddington and the hamlet of Badbury; Liddington Castle is sometimes known as Badbury Castle.

The cornfields end at a gate into a stony lane that descends to the A419. The Ridgeway Path goes north along this road to turn off at the next junction, where it goes east on the road over Wanborough Plain towards the crossing of the M4. We have to keep to the road for a few more yards, to a cross-roads with a pub, 'The Shepherds' Rest'. The road crossing the Ridgeway here is the Ermine Way, a Roman road, which is not to be confused with the better-known Ermine Street running from London to the north; this one comes from Gloucester by way of Cirencester.

We cross the Roman road on to the Bishopstone road, and just beyond the pub turn right through a gap in the hedge, to find ourselves once more on a wide track bordered by trees and bushes, and with the chalk showing underfoot. This is Fox Hill, now prominently marked by a radio tower. The next hill, in less than half a mile, is Charlbury Hill, with an orange-flashing beacon light for the benefit of aircraft. We pass between the 800-ft. summit of this hill and that of Lammy Down to the south, of the same height. The track continues, wide between hedges, with the chalk dazzling in the sun, and descends towards the crossing of a road coming from Bishopstone. On the north side of the track there is a fine example of what I would call a scalloped combe, a deep valley with pleated sides. Near it is a set of good strip lynchets, terraces raised on the hillside, as though for the cultivation of vines—but these terraces face northwards, away from the sun. Lynchets are said to be caused by generations of contour ploughing, but it has always seemed to me that constructions such as these are deliberate, made for some purpose we do not understand. You may see the lynchets by taking the rough track

Approaching Uffington Castle

Top (opposite): White Horse, Uffington (*Aerofilms Ltd.*)

Below (opposite): Dragon Hill, Whitehorse Hill (in foreground, part of the White Horse)

for a short distance in the direction of Bishopstone, or from the Bishopstone road below the red-brick Ridgeway Farm.

At this crossing there is space for the unofficial parking of three or four cars.

The Ridgeway Path leaves the road as a double furrow, but the furrow turns north through a gate while the path continues narrowing to a mere footpath between bushes encroaching from each side. Yet the track here is fundamentally a wide trackway still, for the tree-grown hedges are far apart. This stretch is evidently little used, and this impression is confirmed as the invading bushes are left behind and the noble Ridgeway once more assumes its generous width.

Between this point and the Idstone crossing we pass from Wiltshire into Oxfordshire. The crossing track runs south to Alfred's Castle and Ashdown Park. King Alfred was certainly in this district, for he won a battle at Ashdown, but what he may have had to do with the castle is no more certain than popular legend. Alfred's Castle is a roughly circular single-bank Iron Age enclosure of about $2\frac{1}{2}$ acres, which lay within a larger enclosure, the latter now visible only from the air. The rampart of the inner enclosure was strengthened by sarsen facing-stones, but a number of these were taken in the seven-

teenth century for the building of Ashdown House, a beautiful small mansion (NT), as neat and as symmetrical as a doll's house. Built about 1660 for Elizabeth of Bohemia, Ashdown House stands about 1½ miles south of the Ridgeway.

West of Alfred's Castle is Starveall Farm, one of three with this name between here and the Thames.

After crossing the Ashbury road (B4000) the Ridgeway continues as a wide grassy lane between fences, running parallel, at a distance of about three-quarters of a mile, with the Icknield Way (B4507) which lies to the north and 200 ft. lower. A grove of trees marks Wayland's Smithy, which is reached over a stile in the hedge and over a field. Wayland, the magical smith who made miraculous swords and created for himself a pair of wings with which to escape his enemies, is reputed to have taken refuge here, where, very tamely, he would shoe your horse for you provided you left the money for it and came back later to collect the animal. The cave is in fact a long barrow at least three thousand years older than the legend of Wayland. About 2800 B.C. the barrow was raised over a funerary structure of wood; it was later altered to cover three chambers built of sarsens. You may go into these chambers to stand in the gloom where the dead once lay. Wayland's Smithy is not as impressive as the West Kennett long barrow, but it enjoys the legendary associations that are lacking in the larger structure.

The single bank and ditch of Uffington Castle, one mile from Wayland's Smithy, enclose eight acres. Little excavation has been done; a tentative examination has shown that the banks are or were faced with sarsens.

Below the castle there is a prominent conical hill, with a flat top, and with patches of bare chalk on its flanks. This is Dragon Hill, on which legend says Saint George killed the dragon, its flowing blood poisoning the ground; another legend has it that Uther Pendragon, the father of King Arthur, is buried here. The spectacular hollow, with scalloped sides, near the hill is called the Manger.

It is, however, the White Horse that has made famous the hill on which Uffington Castle stands. You may go down to this remarkable chalk figure, cut probably in the first century B.C. or A.D., to examine the curious shapes in the turf, which, from a distance, make up the finest figure of the chalk downs.

The scarp of Whitehorse Hill is as steep as any along the path. A narrow one-way road hairpins up it to a large car park at the top; the descent brings you to the Woolstone crossroads. Whitehorse Hill is one of the most popular places along the long-distance path, equalled only by Ivinghoe Beacon.

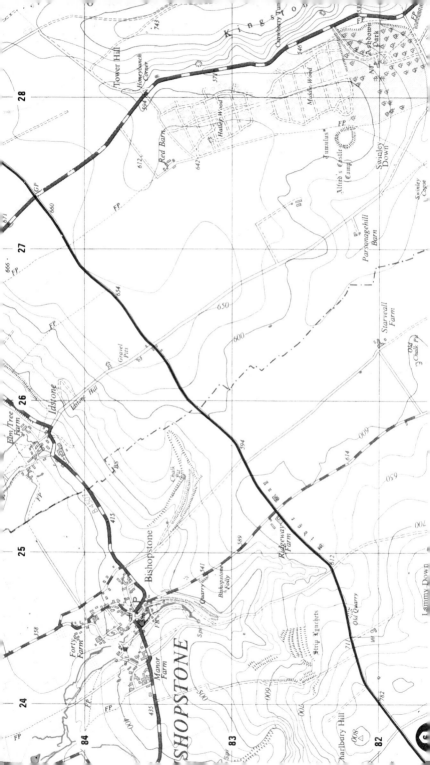

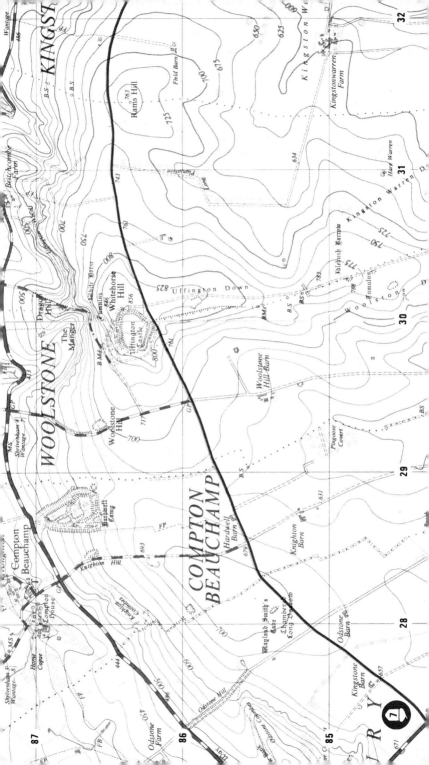

Uffington Castle to Scutchamer Knob

about 11 miles

The Ridgeway passes to the south of Uffington Castle, a little aloof, as though it meant to emphasise that it is the senior by a couple of thousand years of both the castle and the White Horse. It comes from the west as a broad, hedged lane on the chalk, rich with many kinds of wild flowers and blossom. It continues to the east equally broad, or broader, passing the ramparts of the castle a field distant. A green path leaves southward to pass Idlebush barrow, and nearly three miles farther on it passes the Hangman's Stone, on its way into Lambourn. East of the castle the Ridgeway is more open, less hedged, but, chameleon-like, it changes from length to length. Indeed, between Wayland's Smithy and Letcombe Castle we are on one of the most pleasant parts of the long-distance path, sufficiently varied to be interesting, sufficiently open and high to be cool and fresh.

At Whitehorse Hill the track reaches an altitude of 850 ft. It descends a little past the end of Long Plantation, to rise on the slope of Rams Hill and descends again to the Kingston Lisle road. The steep descent from the track to Kingston Lisle is Blowing Stone Hill. The Blowing Stone, in a garden at the foot of the hill, is a holed sarsen, from which a braying trumpet note may be produced by blowing through the holes. It used to be on the Ridgeway, where King Alfred is said to have used it to communicate with his army in the battle of Ashdown against the Danes.

From its junction with the Ridgeway the road from Kingston Lisle runs south over Kingston Warren and Scary Hill to the Seven Barrows. The 'seven' in fact number more than twenty and include bell, bowl, and disk barrows, together with a couple of twin barrows and a long barrow. Crouched skeletons with urns and beakers, ascribed to the second millennium B.C., have been found in these barrows.

The Ridgeway rises to the prominent Hillbarn Clump and drops again to the Collett Bush and the Wixen Bush. These bushes, marked on the map but difficult to distinguish from others on the ground, were evidently once notable points. The track, very rutted in the chalk as it rises past Rubblepit Plantation, is lined with large and healthy thorn bushes. At the summit of the rise the track levels out as a broad, grassy way between fences, passing Hill Barn at 793 ft. The views over the Vale of the White Horse to the distant Cotswolds are expansive—with the cooling towers of the Didcot power station in the middle distance. Whether you regard these structures as handsome or an eyesore is a matter of taste—but see later.

Another industrial object lies ahead near the Ridgeway, a spidery gantry tower with several radar dishes attached. If it looks like Big Brother monitoring your progress, consider that it will be in sight now for several miles. It stands near the junction of two roads coming up from Sparsholt and Childrey and fusing to go south to Lambourn.

The Ridgeway east of this point is a broad beaten way, moderately rough, with downland views on either hand. A sign, 'Private gallops', shows that we are in the exercise country of the racehorse stables at Lambourn. A stile on the north side leads into a field at the head of Crowhole Bottom and the Devil's Punchbowl. This is a convenient place to examine a nascent river valley formed many thousands of years ago, when there was water on the chalk.

For the next few miles the broad track of the Ridgeway is doubled by the equally broad green gallops laid out for the benefit of the race-horses—you may see them early in the morning being exercised. At Folly Clump, a sparse grove of trees, a glance ahead shows what seems to be a sanded track beside the Ridgeway, on the north side. This track, a mile long, is covered, not with sand, but with a thick layer of sawdust and shavings, again for the benefit of the racehorses. It extends to the junction with Gramp's Hill, which rises steeply from the hollow of Letcombe Bassett. Beyond the junction the Ridge-way rises over Parsonage Hill—appropriately enough high above Hell Bottom, the latter a hollow to which a signed footpath drops from Rats Hill. Overlooking it is Letcombe Castle (or Segsbury Camp), at the end of a narrow road from Letcombe Regis. The single and unimpressive bank of this Iron Age fort, revetted with sarsens under the turf, encloses 26 acres. The Ridgeway passes to the south of it.

From Segsbury Barn a gravelled drive and a very rough grassy track run parallel up to the Wantage road (A338), which we follow south for a few yards before again turning eastwards, towards Whitehouse Farm. The lane as far as the farm is metalled, but beyond that the Ridgeway is again a wide and grassy track, and moderately smooth. At a tumulus we come to a point where two wide tracks diverge. The track to the right goes towards Farnborough. Our way, signposted, veers off to the left, towards the Wantage–Newbury road (B4494), which ascends over Middlehill Down. There is ample room for parking at the crossing. Just before this crossing the course of Grim's Ditch joins the Ridgeway from the south, crosses it, and turns east, to run parallel with the way probably as far as the Thames, some 24 miles distant. In places the ditch is apparent, but elsewhere you would need to be a field archaeologist or an airman to find it out.

East of the Wantage road the Ridgeway runs as a broad, tolerably smooth grassy track. In the valley on the north side the six cooling towers and the tall chimney of the Didcot power station now appear near at hand, but they are, in fact, still several miles distant. Nearer to us rises the brick-built complex of the Harwell Atomic Energy Research Establishment. A gravelled drive marked 'Private—to Lockinge' seems to head straight for Didcot. Below the drive a 53

Near Hill Barn above Kingston Lisle

steeplechase course has been constructed round the margin of a field—we are still in racehorse country.

A tall pillar surmounted by a cross and rising from a plinth commemorates Richard Lloyd Lindsay, Baron Wantage, who died in 1901; he fought at the battles of Alma and Inkerman.

Here is one of the smoothest and most level stretches of the Ridgeway, grass-grown and very wide, with woods and clumps of trees to ornament the landscape; but after about a mile and a half the track becomes deeply furrowed once more. Eventually it becomes an avenue between trees, with a row of ashes on the north side and on the south a strip of dense mixed woodland enclosed in barbed wire and marked 'Private'. This wood hides Scutchamer Knob, a Saxon barrow, for more than a thousand years an important landmark. In Colt Hoare's day it was, so he said, 77 ft. high, a giant among barrows. The Danes would have seen it when, after destroying Wallingford, they came up on to the Ridgeway here and turned west to their defeat by Alfred at Ashdown. Today the barrow marks the new county boundary: east from here is Berkshire. The name of 'Scutchamer' appears to derive from Cwicchelmshlaew, the burial place or 'law' of Cwicchelm, a West Saxon king, who according to the Anglo-Saxon Chronicle died in A.D. 593. The name has survived more recognisably in Cuckhamsley Hill.

The narrow lane coming up from East Hendred is surfaced as far as the Ridgeway, where there is space for parking several cars.

56 Purple emperor butterfly on common oak

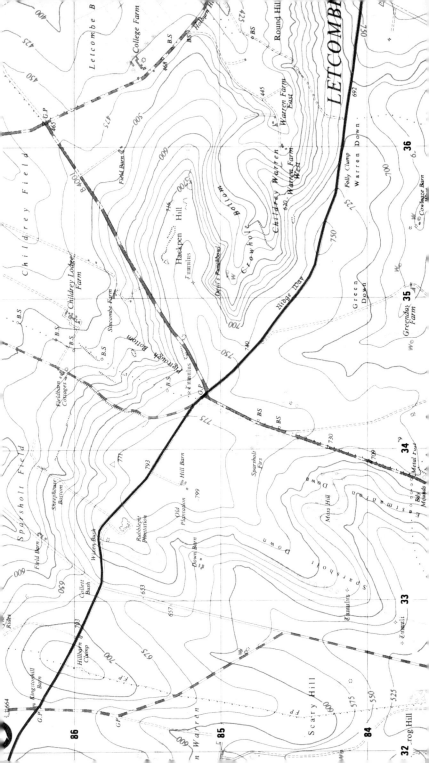

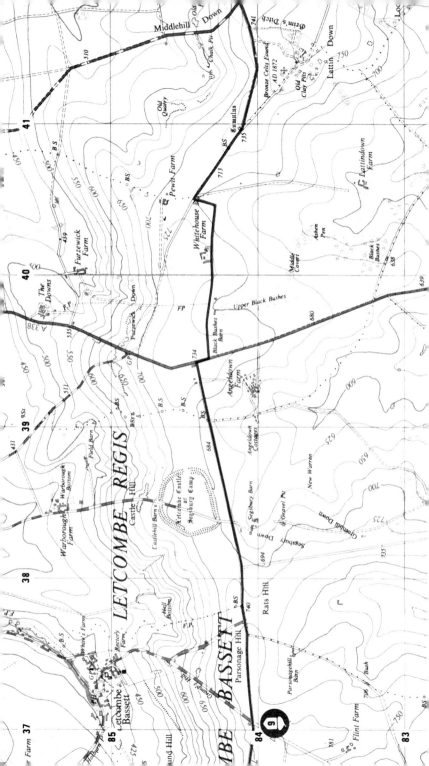

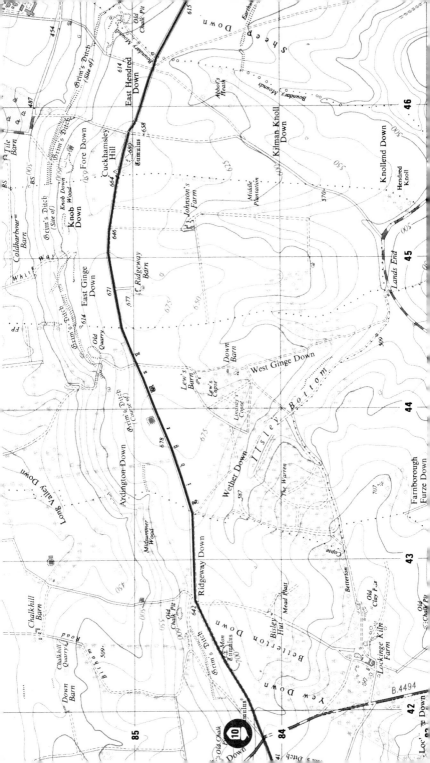

Scutchamer Knob to Streatley

about 10 miles

Eastwards from Scutchamer Knob the Ridgeway continues its broad course over the undulating country of East Hendred Down, with panoramic views to the south and to the north. To the north we now have a clearer view of the many brick buildings of the Harwell Atomic Energy Research Establishment. Founded in 1946 to carry out research into all aspects of atomic energy, it has expanded into many kinds of research on behalf of industry, of medicine, and of science in general. Today only about half of the 5,000 staff are still concerned with improving reactor materials and fuels. The others are employed on work for industry and government, some of which is far removed from nuclear science—environmental pollution, medical engineering, industrial control systems, non-destructive testing, etc. There is even a postal service for resolving problems. The two dome-like buildings standing a little apart from the rest are the research reactors Dido and Pluto, in which some of the experiments take place.

As we pass on over Bury Down the power station at Didcot looms larger and more impressive than Harwell, its six great cooling towers and tall chimney rising high into the air. When there is a mist or heat haze on the plain the towers become ethereal and seem to float insubstantially on a sea and then this great industrial structure might be fit subject for a Japanese painter. In less romantic weather the towers exhibit rather the brutality of modern industry in the countryside, and you may be interested to learn that the Central Electricity Board 'paid close regard to the effect that this project would have upon the general amenities and the natural beauty of the surrounding countryside'. This is why the six cooling towers are placed in two groups of three each, half a mile apart, rather than in one massive clump. What has been done has certainly been done as well as may be, but one can scarcely hide or minimise towers 375 ft. high with a base diameter of 325 ft. Such things are bound to be visible over many miles, a huge area of country.

The station is powered by coal, six million tons of it annually, which comes by rail via Oxford. The cooling towers, like the radiator in a car, serve to cool the water that cools the turbo-generators. The water used for making steam to drive those generators comes partly from the Thames and partly from a borehole down into the reservoirs of the chalk below Compton.

The Ridgeway, in company with the wide, green racehorse gallops,

Harwell Atomic Energy Research Establishment

goes over Bury Down to cross the West Ilsley road, where there is ample parking space. Beyond this point, it stretches into the distance, broad, green, rutted, just as before. As you go along you come within sight of a blue RAC box, which seems to stand incongruously on the ancient way. In fact, it stands at the crossing of the Ridgeway and the busy East Ilsley road, the A34, where a few cars may park. The track rises and falls into the distance eastwards, between cornfields, in company with occasional thorn bushes. The fields appear to suggest good farming country, but a mile to the north stands Skeleton Farm, while to the south of the Ridgeway and farther east is another Starveall. At an altitude of 554 ft. the track crosses Several Down a short distance south of Fox Barrow. The barrow stands above a hollow in which formerly ran a railway. Beyond that there are further good examples of barrows on the slopes of Churn Hill, with yet another one, Churn Knob, on the summit.

We pass through a gate on to a track that soon joins a concrete road looping out from a group of barns labelled 'Agricultural Research Council Experimental Area'. This is part of the council's Institute for Research on Animal Diseases, whose headquarters are to the south in the village of Compton. The institute investigates and seeks cures for diseases not only of farm stock such as cattle, pigs, sheep, and poultry, but also, at times, of mice, guinea-pigs, rabbits, etc.

61

Didcot power station

The margins of the large field opposite the experimental area are laid out as gallops, with indicators in the turf for distances. Hereabouts is a pleasant place to ride or to walk, at least for those who have time to look around. The track seems on top of the world, running in the clear air of the high downs. The Ridgeway is seen far into the distance, dipping into a valley below Blewbury Down and rising beyond towards Lowbury Hill.

We follow the concrete road, ignoring turnings off, until we come to a Ridgeway sign at a crossing, where the concrete goes straight ahead. The sign points east, following the field in which the gallops are. *West-bound travellers, on coming to the crossing, should turn north-west (right) on to the concrete road. This turn needs emphasis because the track straight ahead (south-west) is broad and grassy and looks as though it ought to be the Ridgeway, which it is not.*

The Ridgeway continues beside the gallops eastwards, or east of north-east, distinctly on clay. As you descend the slope of Compton Downs you pass on to old wood shavings, as comfortable for walkers as for horses. Here, when the fields are newly ploughed, you may see how numerous the white flints are in the soil, giving the dark reddish clay a snowy bloom. There are plenty of flints on the track, too.

Ignore a turning south beside a deep trench and continue downhill

to cross a brick bridge over the trench, which in fact is a railway cutting. The railway lines have gone and the trains come no more.

To the north you will see a row of rifle targets of the Churn rifle range. Near them, beyond the railway bridge, a right of way goes back over the fields and passes Lower Chance Farm on the way to Blewbury.

East of the railway bridge, as the Ridgeway, now a hedged lane, begins to climb, a track leaves eastwards to pass north of the summit of Lowbury Hill and join the Fair Mile, a long, straight green way that is a favourite with horse-riders. It leads in two and a half miles to Kingstanding Hill, where it descends past another Starveall Farm to the Icknield Way (A417).

The Ridgeway continues over Roden Downs. The village of Compton is seen over the fields to the south and at the hours the bell of its church sounds over the corn. At a junction of tracks you may turn off to visit Lowbury Hill, on which are an Ordnance Survey triangulation point, a barrow, and the site of a Romano-British temple.

Bushes begin to intrude on the Ridgeway, which changes from a track to a narrow lane. Passing beneath a row of oak trees, it joins at the upper Warren Farm the gravelled farm lane and begins its descent towards the Thames. On the south side a valley develops, with fields speckled with molehills, and among them, clearly outlined on 63 the opposing slope, a rectangular bank enclosing an old field. The pasture gives way to fields of corn, into which the headlands of the grass jut as do promontories into the sea.

The track drops down through a thickly hedged lane, at the foot of which, near the lower Warren Farm, we join a surfaced road. This leads between a medley of houses, mostly middle-class in size and style, to join the A417 and the A329 in about a mile. The A417 is the Icknield Way. It descends below the hump of Lough Down towards Streatley. Lough Down (NT) has ancient field systems, which lie partly on a golf course, but most of the people who come up here come not for archaeology but for the fresh, cool air and the view of the Thames and the Goring Gap.

Streatley takes its name from a Roman road (*strata*) that came along the Icknield Way to cross the river here.

Brown hare with black knapweed

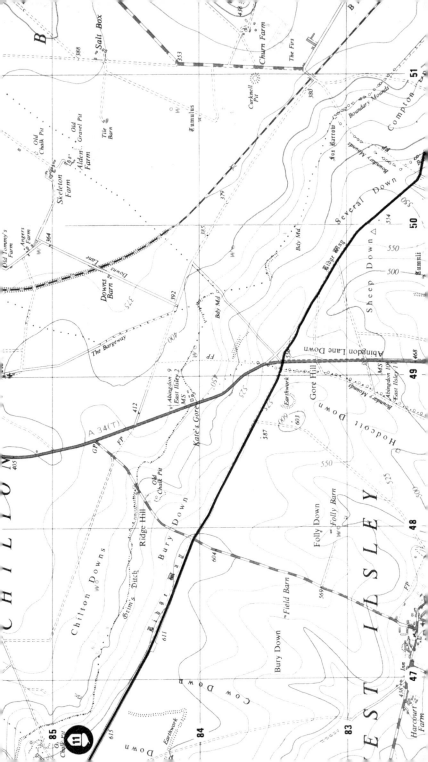

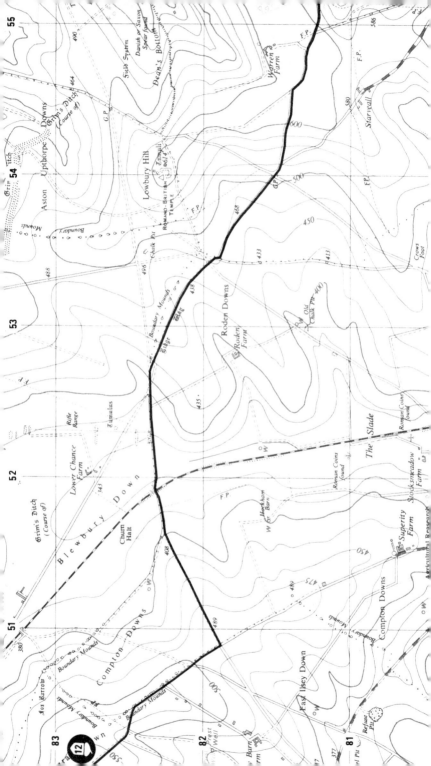

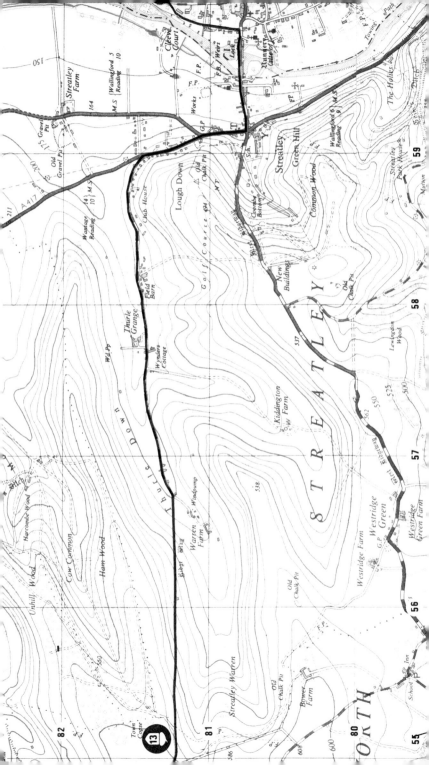

Goring to Swyncombe

about 11 miles

The riverside village of Goring gives its name to the Goring Gap. The gap is not a gorge, but rather a broad opening between the chalk downs of Wessex and the Chiltern Hills. The gap was probably formed in the ice ages. The Thames originally flowed in a different course, north-east towards the Wash. Blocked by ice, the river waters ponded back until they found a weak spot in the chalk hills and overflowed there to form the present course.

Goring has an old inn, the Miller of Mansfield, and a church that in the Middle Ages was the chapel of a nunnery as well as the parish church. The church contains a twelfth-century or thirteenth-century bell, one of the oldest in the county, and a brass of 1375 for Henry Aldrington, with the inscription in Norman French; twenty-five years later, when his wife died, the language was English.

Coming from the river, we take the first turn left, into Thames Road, in which cars may be parked. As a road it is a cul-de-sac, but it is continued by a narrow footpath, from which there are occasional glimpses of the Thames and of boats. At Cleeve, if you wish to be on the ancient track, you may pick up the Icknield Way again; it goes north-east as a metalled road, beside Catsbrain Hill and through Drunken Bottom, to Grim's Ditch, where we shall find it once more— for this is not the route of the long-distance footpath. That path keeps close to the river towards South Stoke, but moves away from the water to pass behind the Leatherne Bottel Hotel, a well-known boating inn with an ancient curative well. Here you will find a contradiction. An official sign indicates a public bridleway ahead, along a pot-holed street, at the entrance to which a sign declares: 'Private Road open to visitors and residents only.' This sign may refer to cars; it cannot refer to walkers and horse-riders, for there is a public right of way. The path leads to the riverside village of South Stoke, which has timbered and thatched cottages, a medieval dove-cot with nests for two thousand birds, and a pleasant old church with ancient glass of the Virgin in a thirteenth-century lancet window.

From the village we pass down a shady lane to the river bank opposite the Beetle and Wedge Hotel, as renowned among river men as is the Leatherne Bottel; 'beetle' in the name is a kind of mallet. We turn north into a field to go along the Thames towpath. The towpath passes beneath Moulsford railway bridge, built by Brunel aslant the river; notice the skewed bricklaying.

Goring-on-Thames (*Aerofilms Ltd.*)

Miller of Mansfield Inn, Goring

Sun-dial, North Stoke

In about a mile along a narrow footpath and over a series of stiles, and finally through what seems to be a private hen-run, we come to the village of North Stoke. From the hen-run we climb a stile beneath a large hawthorn tree into the churchyard. Glance here at the sun-dial in the south wall of the church. It is in the form of a disk held by two hands, with a head projecting above, as though the figure were reaching from inside through the masonry. The church dates from the thirteenth-century and has ironwork of that time on the door. Inside there are highly interesting thirteenth-century and four-teenth-century wall-paintings and a Jacobean pulpit.

Pass round the church tower, with its funny little brick pinnacles, and leave the churchyard beneath the lime-tree-shaded lych-gate, which was given by Dame Clara Butt, the singer, in memory of her son, who died as a boy at Eton; she lived in the village at Brook Lodge.

At the end of the church lane turn left out of the village into a tree-shaded lane, which goes north into Mongewell Park. The park is now the property of Carmel College, a Jewish public school, the buildings of which are modern. Keep straight ahead through the college and take a paved path between railings until you come to a Ridgeway signpost pointing into a narrow band of woodland on the right. The path is not clear and the direction may seem unlikely, but follow the sign and you will find acorn symbols on the tree boles. You

Ewelme Park

come out on to a tarmac drive (a branch of the main drive), crossing
your line. On the other side of this branch drive stand three trees,
which may bear acorn symbols. Cross the drive and go forward,
keeping these trees, all of them, on your *right* hand. You will find a
path, not well worn, along a narrow avenue of beech trees, which
leads out of the park on to the B479. On the far side of this busy road,
which has recently been widened, you will see a stile in a new wooden
fence. Pass through this and you are on the top of the bank of a length
of Grim's Ditch that leads in about four miles to Nuffield. About a
mile from Mongewell it crosses the Icknield Way coming from
Drunken Bottom.

There is an inconsistency here. The Ordnance Survey 1:50,000
map shows the path as running beside and to the south of the bank,
and so does the 2½-inch map; in fact, the path is *on top* of the bank,
where it is well marked. It is classified as a bridleway but riders will
not get along it and even a led horse will not be easy.

The bank is distinctive, up to 10 ft. high, quite straight, and covered
with bushes and trees along its length. Eventually the path descends
from the bank and path and ditch enter woodland. Here Grim's
Ditch becomes more obviously a ditch, a deep and decided furrow,
with the accompanying bank less emphatic. The path sometimes goes
in the bottom of the ditch, sometimes to one side or the other, but
later the stiles are on the south side. You can scarcely get lost, for
you follow the ditch to its end, where you will find a Ridgeway signpost. Follow as indicated northwards, out of the wood and beside a

field, to a stile into the village of Nuffield. From this stile you will have one of your last views of Didcot power station, which has come with us so far. We shall see it at least once more.

We are now only a few steps from Nuffield church, which was built of flint in the thirteenth century. It contains a font, plain except for some unusual lettering, and in the churchyard is a modest but finely lettered slab covering the grave of William Morris, Viscount Nuffield, the motor manufacturer and philanthropist.

Almost opposite the church a stile leads through bushes into a cornfield. When I came this way a narrow trodden chasm through the corn showed the direction clearly.

On the far side of this field we climb a stile on to a golf course. The way across the course is indicated by a series of posts bearing black acorns on a white ground. These posts can be seen one from the other. You cross tees and greens and should do so looking out for your own safety and at the same time treating golfers with the courtesy you expect to receive from them. On the far side of the course we pass between a house and its garage on to the screeching A423, which we have to cross to a gate on the far side.

Beyond a screen of trees we come on to a hillside planted with infant conifers, among which all sorts of wild plants grow luxuriantly, a paradise for botanists and entomologists, though uncomfortable for the walker. However, the way is clear to a stile, which we cross to turn right down beside the fence to another cornfield, also with a chasm through the corn. Beyond another strip of 73 woodland is a third cornfield, in which we turn left for a few yards and then up beside a fence. At the top of the field bear left for ten or twenty paces to a short lane through a thicket of hawthorn bushes. We are now distinctly on the path again. It turns right, round a half-hidden pond, beside which in 1953 a hoard of Roman coins was found.

North of this point there is a large mansion, Ewelme Park. The house, vaguely Elizabethan, is said to be a replica (it doesn't look like it) of a genuine Elizabethan house destroyed by fire in 1913. Sited near the edge of the scarp, the house has marvellous views of the plain, over many cornfields and farmlands interspersed with trees and woods. From here the east-bound traveller will see for the last time the familiar outline of the Didcot power station.

As you pass the house you may be startled by the barking of large dogs and the howling of peacocks: both are usually caged.

We go past the house and turn right, round a large farm building, into a lane climbing between trees. When this comes to a gate into a field we go ahead along the right-hand margin of the field, *not* on the more obvious track to the left. Follow round the far corner of the field and here, on a tree, you will find a painted forked arrow, as though the Ridgeway Path divided. Our way is to the left, and shortly it enters a wood and begins a sharp descent beside a wire fence. At the bottom we climb a stile and cross a field into a wide lane shaded by old beech, chestnut, oak, and elm trees.

Travellers coming from the east will need to watch for the field entrance on their left; it is easy to miss.

We are in the grounds of Swyncombe House. The lane goes up to a wide gate and emerges on to a road opposite Swyncombe church.

The church, which has thirteenth-century windows, is of flint, with evidence of herringbone masonry. There is no tower or steeple. Inside are a plain font—Norman or Early English—a broken thirteenth-century bell known as the Justice Bell, and a pretty eighteenth-century organ.

We pass the rectory above the church and come to a T-junction with a country road, the road between Cookley Green and Ewelme. A visit to Ewelme repays every yard of the $2\frac{1}{4}$ miles it is distant from Swyncombe—for its pretty little square court of almshouses, for its fine fifteenth-century flint church, and above all for the magnificently beautiful and at the same time horrific monument of the Duchess of Suffolk—Alice Chaucer, the poet's grand-daughter.

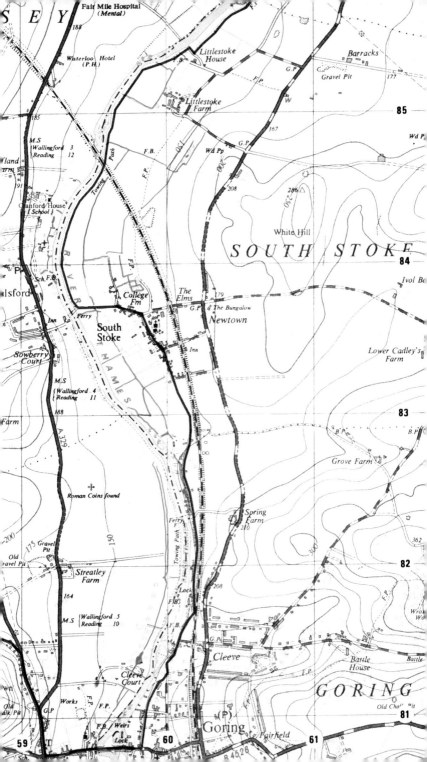

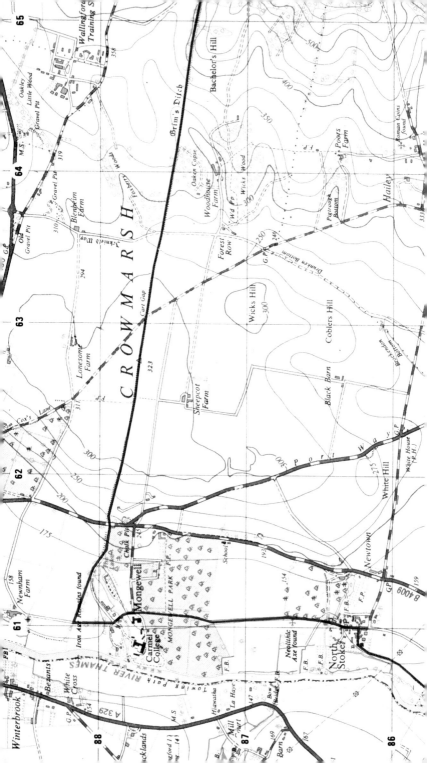

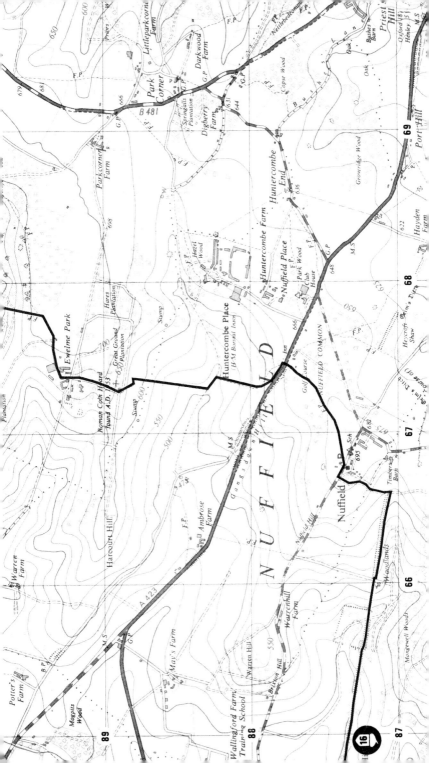

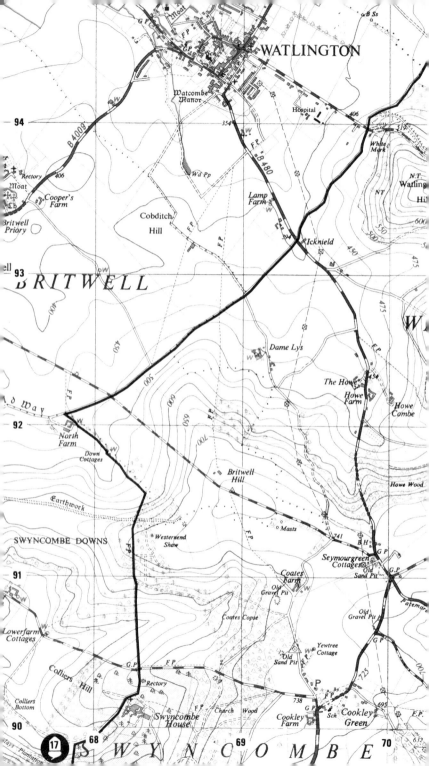

Swyncombe to Bledlow

about 9 miles

There is space to park one or two cars where the Swyncombe lane meets the Ewelme road, and farther back, down the lane, there is room for a few more along the churchyard wall—but note that during service times this space may be occupied.

At the Swyncombe junction we cross the Ewelme road and pass through a gate on to a path descending along the edge of a field. From the bottom of the field the path climbs again, beside a wood, and then enters woodland of beech and conifers on the east end of Swyncombe Downs. As the path descends once more it passes through a linear bank and ditch earthwork, which runs for about a mile from east to west over the down. Both the bank, which is crowned with trees, and the ditch are well defined. The purpose of this work may reasonably be said to be that of a boundary to some property or farm, its date anything from Iron Age to Saxon.

At the foot of the hill we turn along by a tree-inhabited hedge beside a cornfield to North Farm, where we enter a wide green track

Headstone at Swyncombe

79

North Farm country

the Icknield Way once more. This is crossed shortly by the Britwell
road. In the lane each side of the crossing official signs limit parking,
but allow between them so ample a space that one can only suppose
that large numbers of visitors are expected.

For the next three-quarters of a mile the path runs beside broad
cornfields whose female swellings announce the presence of the
chalk beneath the surface. At a junction we come on to a metalled
lane, which turns off south to Dame Alice Farm—no doubt a reference
to Alice Chaucer, the great lady of the district in the fifteenth
century.

At the crossing of the B480 (where signs prohibit parking) we are
only three-quarters of a mile from Watlington. Beside the track rise
the slopes of Watlington Hill (NT), 96 acres of open down and woodland, with a variety of plants and wild life and wide views over
Oxfordshire. In a clearing among the trees high on the hillside is the
'White Mark', an elongated solid triangle cut in the chalk—you will
have to go down towards Watlington and look back if you wish to
see it. The track becomes a broad green way with the chalk showing
through, as it passes beneath the wooded slopes of Pyrton Hill and
Shirburn Hill, which rise about 300 ft. above us.

Between Bald Hill and Beacon Hill the M40 slices through the
downs in a white-walled canyon 70 ft. deep. There was considerable
controversy about the making of this road, but here it is. Its em-
bankments as it leaves the canyon have been planted to cover the

rawness and this is well done. The track goes underneath in a square tunnel that has nothing to offer aesthetically, even if it may prove a convenient shelter in bad weather.

There is generous official parking where the path meets Sheepcote Lane south of Lewknor.

On Beacon Hill north of the M40 lies the Aston Rowant National Nature Reserve, which you may visit on public footpaths and following a nature trail. The habitats range from grass and scrub to mature woodlands on the summit, and among the plants here are various kinds of orchids. You may see fallow deer in the woods, and in an enclosure are brown Soay sheep from the St. Kilda group of the Scottish isles. The reserve borders the National Trust's Aston Wood. Reserve and wood are in the finest Chiltern woodland country, somewhat modified by the coming of the motorway.

Parking is prohibited where the track crosses the Stokenchurch road, and a notice announces that from this point there is no public right of way for wheeled vehicles. Motorists who are tempted to ignore this, for the track here is wide between its hedges, will find that shortly the way becomes rough and progress is barred by iron posts set in concrete.

Grove Farm lies on the slopes to the south, and above it a wireless telegraphy tower, a surrealist object, pops up from the trees on the summit of the hill, looking out over Aston Rowant and the Vale of Aylesbury.

The path near North Farm, Britwell

From this point you may hear two sounds characteristic of this part of the path. One is the clatter of machinery and the other the barking of numerous dogs. The dogs are in kennels on Chinnor Hill and their constant barking can be heard a mile away. The machinery is that of the quarries at Chinnor, where during all working hours caterpillar excavators gnaw at the chalk and large lorries carry the product to the cement factory nearby. The buildings and tall chimneys of this factory soon come in sight. The Ridgeway Path now truly stands on a ridge, for it runs along an unexcavated line between a quarry on the left and a quarry on the right. A tunnel under the path communicates between one quarry and the other. The thick woods of Oakley Hill form a backdrop to the white amphitheatre of the quarry on the south side. The Chinnor cement factory is the first large-scale industry we have encountered since Didcot.

There is space at the Chinnor crossing for the unofficial parking of a few cars.

Along the slopes of the tree-covered Steppinghill the path changes character, to become a simple country cart track, with white trails of the chalk running among trees and scrub and thorn. Below Wain

Cement works at Chinnor seen from the path

Hill it dwindles to a narrow footpath.

On Wain Hill among the trees, is Bledlow Cross, cut in the chalk. Measuring 75 ft. from side to side, with arms 15 ft. wide, the cross is of unknown origin; it may be no older than the seventeenth century.

A series of tumuli extends along the hill from Chinnor, terminating in the Cop on Wain Hill. The Cop was opened in 1937, when fragments of beakers were found, together with objects ranging from the bronze age to the Saxon period. North of the hamlet of Hempton Wainhill a prosperous Roman or Romano-Briton built a villa in the second century A.D., on a site where an impermeable stratum brings the water of the Wainhill Spring conveniently to the surface.

The Chinnor Hill nature reserve of the Berkshire, Buckingham-shire, and Oxfordshire Naturalists' Trust (BBONT) lies on the wooded slope above Chinnor, rising to Hempton Plain on the summit, at 800 ft. Juniper, yew, whitebeam, and various deciduous trees grow here, and you may see frog orchids and carline thistles. Sheep are grazed to control the scrub. There is a nature trail.

At Hempton Wainhill the few houses of the hamlet line the path. We pass close beside one of them and turn its corner to walk along 83 its front. There is a wide white-painted gate opposite the front door, leading to a track to Bledlow, but this is not our way. We keep along the front of the house, respecting its doorstep, and down beside a trimmed box hedge. You may see some unusual flowers here, but they are not wild and you are asked not to pick them.

We come now to one of the prettiest sections of the track, where a lane hedged on one hand winds along the indented foot of a wooded hillside. In the shade beneath the trees beech leaves gleam on the dark reddish-brown of the loam; here, when the sun is hot, is a pleasant place to be, cool and quiet. A variety of wild plants flourish beside the path. As we climb a steep, deep combe develops on the left side, its slopes planted with sapling trees, under whose tender canopy the light is tinged green.

We come out on to a hedged lane, the Icknield Way, which goes towards Princes Risborough. Here, for a while, we leave the ancient track, which we have followed since we entered it at North Farm between Swyncombe and Britwell, for within a few steps we find a Ridgeway signpost pointing over a stile into a field on our right. The stile is the first of a pattern of which we shall meet several; it has an unusually broad top rail, ideal for sitting on, and here we pause to consider the next section.

Badger and elderberry

84 HT

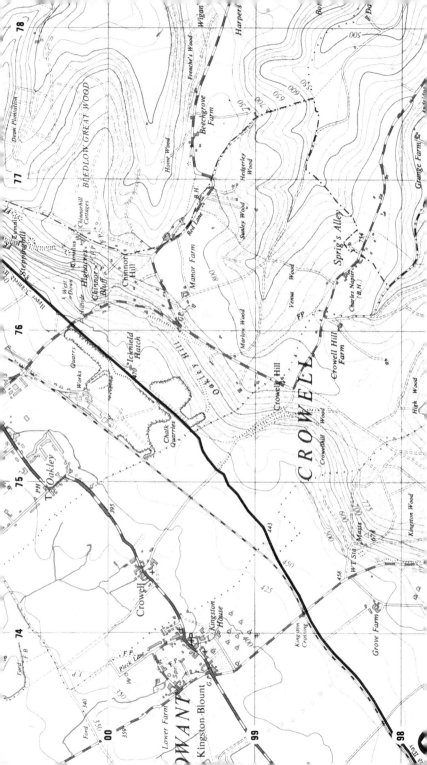

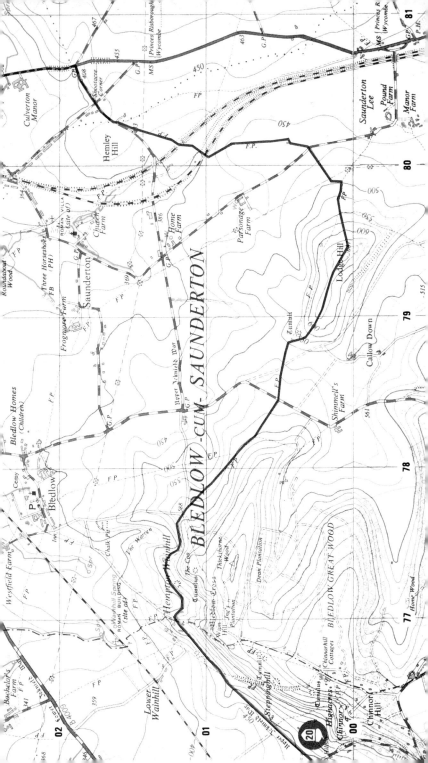

Bledlow to Cock's Hill

about 12 miles

There is no access for vehicles to this part of the Upper Icknield Way where we sit resting on our stile, and therefore no parking at this point, but Bledlow village lies only half a mile away to the north.

The stile gives access to a field in which there is no apparent path except for a white blaze up a slope, starting some distance away to the left. This blaze is a snare and probably a cattle-trod—it will lead you away from the line you want. Our direction lies to a point below the trod, where a hedge forms an angle. We follow this hedge over a faint path pocked with rabbit and badger diggings, to a stile, on the left, marked with an acorn. This leads into a field, with a path along the hedge (now on our right) to the Bledlow road. Here there is space to park three cars, uncomfortably, on a raised verge.

The stile on the east side of this road gives a good view of Lodge Hill rising from cornfields, its slopes dotted with scrub. The path may be seen crossing two fields towards it, and then climbing up the west flank of the hill, so there is no problem of wayfinding here; in any case the path is clearly waymarked. You pass a tumulus on your left and climb the steep but not long pull up on chalk, which gives way to soft turf on the top. The views from the crest are worth the climb. You look over Princes Risborough and its brick outskirts to the scarp of Whiteleaf Hill—which is on our way towards Ivinghoe—while to the north patterned fields and hedges stretch for miles into the misty distances of the Vale of Aylesbury. The view to the south would also be attractive if it were not ravaged by the presence of a large urban rubbish tip—there must be few tips that stand so prominently and so high in such lovely country.

A series of Ridgeway concrete 'plinths' or signs, with arrows on them, show the route across the hill, where there is no clearly marked path, though in practice you may wander freely over much of the hill top (except for the areas marked 'Private'). The signs lead to a stile where the hill begins to descend, and from here you may look ahead at the route of the path down the hillside to a road, across this and over a field, passing a small farm cottage, and then up the slope of Hemley Hill towards Princes Risborough. Let us follow it in more detail beyond the cottage in the field. The path leads to a stile, beyond which is a neglected corner thick with nettles, brambles, 88 wild roses, and other less well-defended weeds—a stick is useful here,

Timber-frame at Princes Risborough

to beat your way through. We escape from this by another stile, and continue beside a field alongside a hedge of hawthorns and crab-apples. Two more stiles and we are on a railway line, which should be crossed with caution since it is still in use. Beyond this we go ahead until a white-painted stile comes in sight on the skyline above a field. Here we cross a second railway line, but this one is in a deep and spectacular cutting, which ends beneath our feet, where the train plunges into a short tunnel on its way to Oxford.

Beyond the line a footpath to the right runs along the top of the cutting to Loosley Row. Our way lies ahead over the corn to a junction with a road, which in a few yards crosses a cross-roads at Shootacre Corner, and goes on to a junction with the A4010 south of Princes Risborough.

From this point a temporary route is in operation so follow the A4010 north for about half a mile—happily, this busy road has a footpath beside it—to a lane turning off to the east, marked 'Upper Icknield Way'. We follow this lane and in about three-eighths of a mile, at a stile on the right coming up from Pyrtle Spring, we are once more on the approved route. Carry on straight ahead to a street lined with modern houses. Cross this street and pass between houses on the far side into a lane that presently passes a football field and comes out at the foot of the slopes of part of Whiteleaf Hill. We climb this hillside north-east through scattered stands of ragwort and thistles to a Ridgeway sign standing beside a stile giving on to a road. Do *not* pass over this stile, but turn to your left (north) alongside a screen of old 89 thorn trees remaining from a former hedge. Pass through this screen to a fence beneath trees and follow this fence *left* through a stile to a gate leading on to the Whiteleaf road, which comes steeply up the scarp, overhung by trees. The Ridgeway is signed through the wood on the opposite side of this road. (A new route is being considered for this section so watch out for signposts.)

A little higher up the hill, out of sight of the path, is the Bucks. County Council's Whiteleaf car park and picnic site (with a low boom to keep out caravans and lorries). This park is a convenient place from which to visit all parts of Whiteleaf Hill.

You may lose your way in the wood, but not if you keep within sight of a paling fence on your right hand, which will lead you to a kind of kissing gate. Pass through this gate and the way is then clear down a wooded hillside, a beautiful walk. You pass, unseen, another chalk figure, the Whiteleaf Cross, similar to the Bledlow Cross, but larger, measuring about 80 ft. across; it probably dates from the eighteenth century. If you wish to see it properly you will have to go down on to the plain and look back. Helleborine grows in these woods.

At the foot of the hill we join a lane coming in from the left. *West-bound travellers should note that this turning, to the left for them, is not obvious, even though marked with a Ridgeway plinth.*

The lane debouches beside the Plough Inn and we turn along the front of this inn to the Cadsdean or Cadsden road. *Here west-bound walkers coming up the Cadsdean road must not miss the side-road on the right leading to the inn. The path continues behind the inn.*

There is parking higher up the road, on Longdown Hill.

From the Plough turning, our way lies down the hill, to find, at the foot, a Ridgeway sign on the left pointing across the road into an easily overlooked opening to a path beside a garden gate, on the right or east side. This exceedingly slender path climbs steeply between the wire fences of gardens equally steep, beneath trees, to come out at the top into a field beside a Ridgeway plinth. Continue straight ahead over the rise of the field and shortly you will see another concrete Ridgeway plinth on the far side in a corner of a hedge. A few feet beyond this, in among bushes, rises a Ridgeway signpost. Follow its direction through hawthorn and other thorn scrubland and in twenty yards or so turn left to a stile marked by an acorn. The way is now plain along the slopes of Pulpit Hill to Chequers Knap, which, with Happy Valley lower down the scarp, is an SSSI—a site of special scientific interest, for its wild life, notably of the chalk flora and the related butterflies. We cross the line of a rifle range, whose butts are seen as earthworks on the right. Above the butts there is an Iron Age camp or small fort, with a double bank and ditch and an entrance on the south-east side 75 ft. wide.

Beyond the butts a high stile marked with acorns leads into a lane, and a few yards beyond this another stile, in the wire fence on the left, leads into a field. The path is not now obvious, but go ahead slightly right, down to and across a long earthwork ditch to a wire fence skirting the head of a deep combe or gorge filled with trees. Turn right along this fence up to a stile and an iron farm gate, from

which the path through a cornfield is distinctly marked.

We are now in the Chequers estate, in which is the Prime Minister's country house. As we pass across the main drive, only a couple of 'Private' notices protect the house—or so it seems, but trespass in the estate and see what happens to you! I dare say policemen will spring out of the rabbit holes. No one will accost you if you follow the signed route.

Chequers is a mid-sixteenth-century mansion with ball-topped gables and large mullioned and transomed windows. Though a number of alterations were made inside by its last private owner, Lord Lee of Fareham, the exterior is largely original. Lord Lee gave the house and estate to the nation in 1921 as a country home for Prime Ministers. The gift was not without opposition—Lord Haldane seemed to think that the unaccustomed luxury of such a country house would do harm to Prime Ministers sprung from the middle classes!

Beyond Chequers, to the north, is another of the several Beacon Hills on or near our route. Below this is the motte and bailey earthwork known as Cymbeline's Castle, from a legend that the ancient British king of Shakespeare's play had a palace or castle here. The neighbouring villages of Great and Little Kimble also carry the name of Cymbeline.

Coming out of the Chequers estate, we cross one of the durable Chequers iron stiles to a road and a Ridgeway signpost pointing up a gravel drive between trees. We soon turn left in a wood on to a long, straight walk, tree-shaded, the Long Walk of Long-walk Wood. *Travellers coming from the east will find their turning off this walk not obvious and should watch for it at a point marked by a narrowing of the Long Walk.* The Long Walk is floored with clay and in wet weather this is adhesive. At the end of the Walk a turn left at a Ridgeway sign brings us to a black and white iron bar across the opening to a surfaced road. *This Ridgeway sign is principally for the benefit of west-bound travellers, but it cannot be seen from the surfaced road; these travellers should look for the iron bar, pass beside or under it, and then follow the Ridgeway signpost direction.*

We descend a yard or two on the surfaced road to a signpost opposite one of the lodges of Chequers Park and turn right along the road towards Butler's Cross. Within a few feet we take a right turn into a leafy lane marked by a sign 'Public footpath and bridleway' and an acorn. We follow the path through woodland on the side of a second Lodge Hill to a barred gate. Just beyond this we turn right, through trees, and up the steepest ascent on the whole route of the long-distance path—it is like climbing a roof, but a roof that is slippery because the ground is clay. There is not much trouble getting up, but there may be for those coming down, especially after rain. (At time of writing this was the signposted route, but a diversion is proposed through Linton's Wood and across Lodge Hill, to avoid this steep hill. Both routes are shown on the map on page 96.)

At the top of the rise we turn along a clear path towards a tall pillar monument on the summit of the National Trust's Coombe Hill, which, at 852 ft., is the highest viewpoint on the Chilterns. There are convenient seats for those who wish to enjoy the view. It seems limitless, coming round from Pulpit Hill, with Chequers at its foot,

Chequers

and northwards over the fields and farms towards Aylesbury. The tall monument, which may be seen afar from points in the vale, is a memorial to the dead of the South African War. It is apparently in a dangerous condition.

Coombe Hill is an sssi, contrasting the calcifuge flora of the clay-with-flints summit with the chalk-loving flora of the slopes. A nature trail helps towards the perception of the contrast.

Up here on the hill you may meet a tribe of goat-like brown and white sheep with two pairs of horns—or as many as six horns. The lambs are black and white. These are Jacob sheep, of a breed believed to be as old as the Book of Genesis, the 'sheepe with little spots and great spots' mentioned in the 1599 edition of the Bible. A society has been founded to improve the breed (the flock on Coombe Hill belongs to the secretary). The society's circular says of Jacob sheep: 'Bright-eyed and alert, they are intelligent, friendly, and capable of inspiring great affection from their owners.'

The summit of Coombe Hill is a favourite place of relaxation for the people of the district and in good weather you are certain to meet many people there.

By turning east round the monument and passing over the down, we come to a stile from which the mile-long descent to Wendover is begun, an easy and delightful walk on the descent, a not too steep or too breathless a walk on the ascent. We join the Butler's Cross road to descend into the little town of Wendover.

We go straight ahead down through the town, past a number of old pubs, and at the bottom of the street, in front of an ugly clock tower, we turn right into Heron's Walk, a paved lane, passing a brick and flint school and then alongside a stream. It leads to the church of St. Mary, which was built of flint in the early fourteenth century; this contains a brass of William Bradschawe, d. 1537, and his wife, with their nine children and twenty-three grandchildren. We follow left round the churchyard, on a surfaced road, to a junction by the inn at Wellhead. Here we cross the road and take a lane between hedges, which leads in three-quarters of a mile to Boswells Farm. There is unofficial parking for a few cars in the lane *before* you come to the first Ridgeway signpost. Boswells is a neat and efficient-looking modern farm. We cross its tree-lined drive and go through a large swing gate opposite into a lane in a wood. Where the track bears left we go straight forward along a narrower path, and past a Ridgeway sign pointing back the way we have come. Leave the sign on your right.

Soon the path comes to a division, to the left along level or descending ground, to the right on an overgrown trail climbing aslant a hillside planted with young conifers—the latter is our way and an acorn stencilled on a tree-bole here and there confirms the route. We are on clay nearly all the time and in wet weather it is evident—there are tractor-cut morasses occasionally. The path runs along Cock's Hill above a valley over which there are views of the wooded slopes of Boddington Hill, where, hidden among the 93 trees, there is a large hill-fort of the Iron Age. At what seems to be the end of this stretch of the path we turn left for half a dozen steps down the hill to find a gate on the right marked with acorns. We pass along by Hale Wood into a wide grassy lane much indented by the hooves of horses. This leads to a five-barred gate opening on to the single-track surfaced road coming up the hill from Hale. The Ridgeway Path dives into the woods on the other side of this road.

Jacob sheep

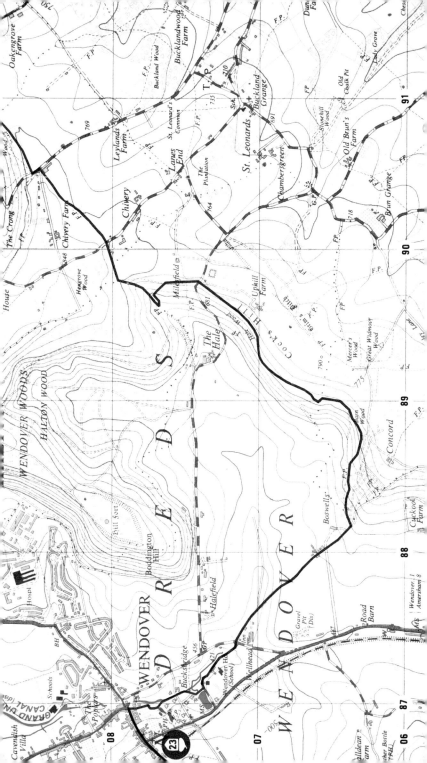

Cock's Hill to
Ivinghoe Beacon

about 10 miles

The wood into which the path passes from the road is thick and dim
and the way through is not self-evident—you must look for the acorn
signs. These lead to a gorge 10 or 12 ft deep, with a wet path in the
bottom, an example of how wear and weather, working through many
centuries, can erode a path deep down into the earth to reach the
chalk bedrock; it demonstrates also how thick the overlying layers
of clay and loam may be.

There is a signed horse trail in this wood.

We climb up through the trees to come out on a rough lane and
then to a surfaced road. On the far side of this road a stile passes
through the hedge into a field in which there is no plain path—go
ahead with the fence or hedge on your right hand, to a second stile.
There is again no obvious path, but in the distance you will see an
iron electricity pylon. You should make for this pylon, and in the
far corner of the field, amid a clutter of nettles and old farm vehicles,
you should find a Ridgeway signpost. It brings us on to a minor
surfaced road, which, to the north, descends the Chiltern scarp in a
hairpin known as the Crong. We do not go so far, however—we turn
off the road into a wood, round the foot of the pylon, where we find
white acorns on the tree-boles, together with shapeless yellow blobs.
The path now runs for about a mile along the southern margin of
Northhill Wood and Pavis Wood, which cover the slope of the scarp
with a medley of trees, mostly hardwoods. In Pavis Wood we bear off to
the right on a footpath that soon joins the Hastoe road where that
road makes a right-angled bend.

We now follow the surfaced road through the hamlet of Hastoe to
join the Cholesbury–Tring road at Hastoe Cross. On the far side of
this road a signpost marked 'Wigginton—footpath' points through a
field gate. A straight course on a shingled drive passes Wick
Farm—nearly parallel, at a quarter of a mile distance, with a stretch
of one of the many Grim's Ditches. The drive descends towards an
estate of recently built bungalows. Look for a Ridgeway signpost on
the left. It points into a cornfield immediately behind the first
bungalow, and for some distance now the path runs alongside a row of
back gardens. The plants you may see here include escapes from those
gardens.

Steps Hill and Ivinghoe Beacon from stile on Ivinghoe road

We pass from the cornfield round a wild, nettle-filled corner and out of this along the edge of woodland on the borders of Tring Park. An iron swing gate precedes by a few steps a stile that brings us into a short stretch of private road that ends in an entrance to the park. At the other end the private road comes to a public road, on the far side of which there is a stile.

Travellers coming from the east will find a forbidding notice facing them at the entrance to the private road: they should not be deterred, for there is a right of way. At the end of this road do not miss the stile on your left by going ahead into Tring Park.

(The section from Pavis Wood is temporary. It is possible that the route will be changed in the future, so watch out for signposts.)

The stile on the public road gives us our first view of the hills on the last stage of our journey. The bare grey muzzle of Ivinghoe Beacon projects, in the distance, from the scarp that includes Pitstone Hill and Steps Hill. Where we stand we are not in fact much lower than the summits and the prospect seems as enticing as it is easy.

Also in the view is a large factory with five tall chimneys rising out of a landscape that seems to hang in the air. Nearer at hand is the large cutting of the Tring by-pass, the A41(M). These large enterprises modify one's enthusiasm for the view.

Crossing the field we come to two stiles, set together at a right-angle and giving access to two fields. A bull is occasionally run in one or other of them so choose the safer field. *A similar arrangement exists for eastbound walkers.* Beyond them we keep a fence or hedge on our left 99

White Lion from Steps Hill

as far as the Wigginton road. The bend in this road going down the scarp to the north is called the Twist. We turn away from it, up the narrow road to the south, and in a short distance find on our left a stile marked with acorns. It leads to a path that descends to a crossing over the new motorway and shortly afterwards to the A41. The A41, today a fast and busy road, is the Roman Akeman Street. Fortunately, it has good grass verges, for having crossed this road we turn right along it for a short distance, and then left beside the grounds of Pendley Manor (a centre for adult education). The path goes beside a field that was growing beans when this book was written and will probably be sown to corn in after years.

We turn left on to a surfaced road to cross the Grand Union Canal by the road bridge. When this was written an official route had not been agreed so a temporary route was waymarked. This follows a street lined with houses and crosses the railway on the bridge above Tring station. After the bridge, continue along the Aldbury road, past the first junction, and bear left shortly at a Ridgeway signpost, and then left again at a junction of footpaths. In a little

Pitstone Mill

more than a quarter of a mile you will join a tree-shaded lane leading to Aldbury Nowers.

From this point begins one of the most glorious walks to be experienced along the whole course of the long-distance path, extending to the summit of Ivinghoe Beacon. We climb up through woodland and grassland, sometimes over clear going, sometimes through a wilderness of grasses and other plants chest high, where in season you may regale yourself with wild raspberries, and always with a wide-spreading view over the plain to the east and north. True, the view contains the huge building of the Tunnel Cement Company's Pitstone works, which is no less, and perhaps no more, obtrusive than the atomic centre at Harwell and the power station at Didcot. Pitstone Hill, open and clear, is an excellent place to sit and examine the view, a remarkable element of which is the quarries of this Pitstone factory. The excavations, begun in 1937, now extend over large areas, level-floored, and so vast that from our view the depth seems small. The chalk and marl extracted, when mixed 101

together, form the main constituent for the manufacture of Portland cement.

North of the quarries is the village of Pitstone, with its thirteenth-century to fifteenth-century church, and north of that again a post windmill, complete with its sails, stands in the middle of a cornfield. The mill, which is the property of the National Trust, is dated 1627, but it was probably rebuilt later than that date, re-using the original timbers. It was restored from 1963 onwards by voluntary labour and it is now in working order. It is open to visitors on certain days.

North of the windmill the village of Ivinghoe spreads along its streets its glow of red brick, with the centrally towered church in front.

On the hill some irregular earthworks catch the eye. They include a long ditch aslant the slope, which you may follow towards the hill top and a wire fence leading northwards. We descend Pitstone Hill to the Ivinghoe–Aldbury road and turn north along this to a stile on the east side of the road. There is an official car park behind the hedge opposite this stile.

The stile gives a long, inviting view of the next stage, which goes along a chalky field to climb through sparse scrub and bushes up the scarp. On the way up we pass round the head of a deep valley, Incombe Hole, from which the convex side of Steps Hill rises, its many scattered bushes throwing long shadows in the afternoon sun.

You can scarcely go astray over Steps Hill, not even if you walk with your eyes in the air looking at the gliders you are likely to see if the weather is suitable. Pass over the hill and glance to the east as you descend towards a road: $2\frac{1}{2}$ miles away, towards Whipsnade a large, modern chalk-cut figure of a lion shines on the hillside.

A glitter of glossy painted metal announces the National Trust's new car park for Ivinghoe Beacon, up in a field, where in warm weather you may find a gaudy ice-cream van. We descend to where cars used to park beside the road at the foot of the ascent to the Beacon. The Trust is concerned about erosion of the turf cover of the chalk, and you will see here that their concern is justified. You are asked by notices to avoid the worn areas. White trails of chalk climb the hill towards the summit. There you are likely to find a number of people around the Ordnance Survey triangulation column and around the direction indicator, from which someone has stolen the brass disk. On a fine day wireless-controlled model planes and gliders will be swooping and circling above your head, for this is a favourite place for the enthusiasts of this sport. Silent witnesses of the past include two bowl barrows and an iron-age hill-fort.

The view is remarkable, extending round the full 360 degrees of the horizon. A great deal of what you see to the south and east belongs to the National Trust, round to Moneybury Hill and the monument to the 3rd Earl of Bridgwater above Aldbourne—he was the 'father' of canal development in the eighteenth century. To the east is that white lion near Whipsnade. To the north lies the village of Edlesborough, with its large church standing apart at Church

H

End; the tall west tower rises from a tumbled graveyard on a hill
and it looks as though the church was built on a prehistoric earthwork—a thing by no means unprecedented. You may be able to make
out, beyond the church, the large sixteenth-century barn of Church
Farm. To the west of the Beacon is extensive farmland, while to the
south are the scarped hillsides along which we have come on this
the last of the stages of our long-distance path from Overton Hill
in Wiltshire. Below us two roads come from the south-west, the Upper
Icknield Way and the Lower Icknield Way, seasonal tracks of
prehistoric travellers; now each is a surfaced modern road. At
Ivinghoe they unite and the Icknield Way, now neither upper nor
lower, continues north-east as a single road, the B489, towards
Dunstable.

From any point to which our view extends the Beacon may in turn
be seen. No place could be more effective to light a signal fire, for
whatever cause of rejoicing or alarm there may have been in the two
long millennia since men of the Iron Age built their fort on the summit
of the hill.

Atop Ivinghoe Beacon

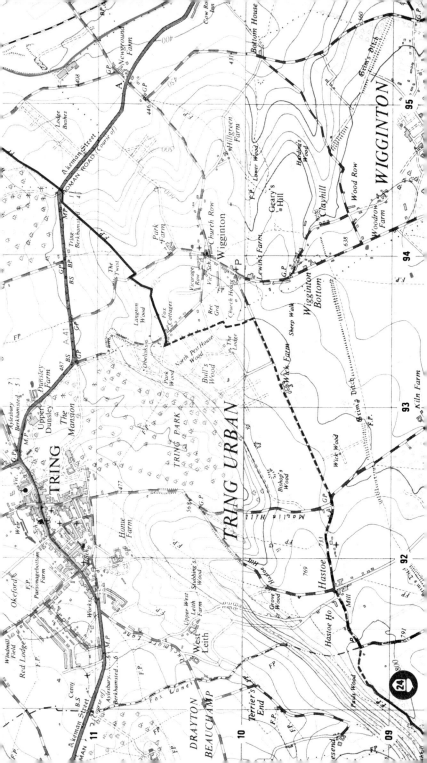

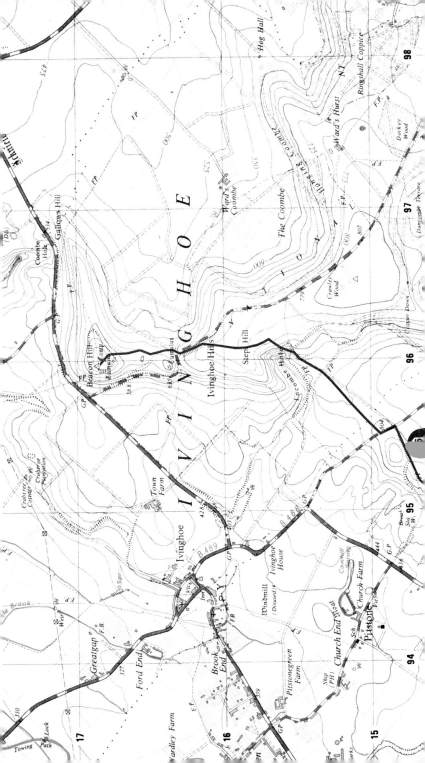

Accommodation

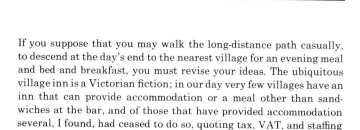

If you suppose that you may walk the long-distance path casually, to descend at the day's end to the nearest village for an evening meal and bed and breakfast, you must revise your ideas. The ubiquitous village inn is a Victorian fiction; in our day very few villages have an inn that can provide accommodation or a meal other than sandwiches at the bar, and of those that have provided accommodation several, I found, had ceased to do so, quoting tax, VAT, and staffing problems as factors that made it no longer worth while. Some places that do provide bed and breakfast do not provide an evening meal, or do not provide an evening meal on Sundays.

Most villages have a pub where you may have a sandwich with your drink. An occasional pub as, for example, the Red Lion at Whiteleaf, bars hikers. The landlord presumably recognises a hiker by his rucksack and his big boots.

There are Youth Hostels convenient for the route at Streatley, at Bradenham (4½ miles distant), at Lee Gate (2½ miles distant), and at Ivinghoe. There are other hostels, but less convenient, at Oxford and at Inglesham. Oxford, however, may be used as a centre for reaching various parts of the path by bus. Details of membership and opening times can be obtained from the Youth Hostels Association, Trevelyan House, 8 St. Stephens Hill, St. Albans, Herts. AL1 2DY.

It is advisable to book accommodation ahead, especially in summer, and at week-ends in any season.

A short book list

British Regional Geology: London and the Thames Valley. Her Majesty's Stationery Office, London. A handbook covering the whole length of the path.

Field Archaeology: some notes for beginners. Her Majesty's Stationery Office, London.

Archaeology in the Field by O. G. S. Crawford. Phoenix House, London.

Wessex by Peter Fowler. Regional Archaeologies Series. Heinemann Educational Books.

Ancient Trackways of Wessex by H. W. Timperley and Edith Brill. Phoenix House, London.

The Green Roads of England by R. H. Cox. Methuen, London. A somewhat erratic book but interesting.

Neolithic and Bronze-Age Collections in the Devizes Museum by F. K. Annable and D. D. A. Simpson. Wilts. Archaeological and Natural History Society.

The Icknield Way by Edward Thomas. 1913.

An Autumn Effect by R. L. Stevenson. An essay on the country between Wendover and Tring.

White Horses and Other Hill Figures by Maurice Marples. Country Life.

Prehistoric England by Grahame Clark. Batsford.

Tom Brown's Schooldays by Thomas Hughes. 1857.

The Scouring of the White Horse by Thomas Hughes. 1859.
These two books describe the countryside in the neighbourhood of Uffington and the White Horse.

The Wild Flowers of Britain and Northern Europe by Richard Fitter, Alastair Fitter, and Marjorie Blamey. William Collins.

The Story of my Heart by Richard Jefferies. 1883.

The Oldest Road: an exploration of the Ridgeway by J. R. L. Anderson. Wildwood House, London.

Bed and Breakfast and Bus Guide. Ramblers' Association. Annual.

Campsites of Britain. Charles Letts. Annual.

The Country Code

Guard against all risk of fire

The countryside is not simply landscape and fresh air; it is the countryman's workshop and his livelihood. A careless match or a cigarette stub can do immense and costly damage. Make sure that matches and cigarettes are extinguished. Take care also with picnic stoves.

Fasten all gates

There are few gates on the long-distance path. Make sure to close them behind you.

Keep dogs under proper control

Dogs chasing farm animals may harm them and cause abortion of their young. Make sure it does not happen. Do not throw sticks or stones into cornfields and send your dog in to recover them; the dog will do a lot of damage to the corn.

Keep to the paths across farm land

There is no need to trespass anywhere along the path. Where you have to go through cornfields keep in single file.

Avoid damaging fences, hedges and walls

There is no need to go through a single fence or hedge anywhere along the path other than by a stile or a gate.

Leave no litter

You would be an unusual person if you did not mind seeing litter, old tins, and broken glass in the countryside. Don't add to it yourself. It is not only unsightly, it can and does cause damage and injury.

Safeguard water supplies

If there is little opportunity to pollute water supplies along the Ridgeway Path you should none the less keep this tenet in mind in relation to any you encounter—which includes cattle troughs in fields.

Protect wild life, wild plants and trees

A great deal of the charm of the countryside lies in the plants that grow there. Admire them, examine them, identify them, but do not
pick or uproot them.

Go carefully on country roads

Country roads may be quiet—but expect the unexpected. There may be a cow around that bend or a sheep asleep on the warm tarmac, or a pony ambling along; or ramblers walking. It can be dangerous to think of country roads as deserted.

Respect the life of the countryside

The farmer is a skilled man doing a difficult and multifarious job. Don't interfere with his machinery or his installations, and leave farm animals alone.

Kestrel

Sparrowhawk

Common Buzzard